D1607741

Fukushima and the Privatization of Risk

DOI: 10.1057/9781137343123

Other Palgrave Pivot titles

Majia Holmer Nadesan: **Fukushima and the Privatization of Risk**

Ian I. Mitroff, Lindan B. Hill, and Can M. Alpaslan: **Rethinking the Education Mess: A Systems Approach to Education Reform**

G. Douglas Atkins: **T.S. Eliot, Lancelot Andrewes, and the Word: Intersections of Literature and Christianity**

Emmeline Taylor: **Surveillance Schools: Security, Discipline and Control in Contemporary Education**

Daniel J. Hill and Daniel Whistler: **The Right to Wear Religious Symbols**

Donald Kirk: **Okinawa and Jeju: Bases of Discontent**

Sara Hsu: **Lessons in Sustainable Development from China & Taiwan**

Paola Coletti: **Evidence for Public Policy Design: How to Learn from Best Practices**

Thomas Paul Bonfiglio: **Why Is English Literature? Language and Letters for the Twenty-First Century**

David D. Grafton, Joseph F. Duggan, and Jason Craige Harris (eds): **Christian-Muslim Relations in the Anglican and Lutheran Communions**

Anthony B. Pinn: **What Has the Black Church to Do with Public Life?**

Catherine Conybeare: **The Laughter of Sarah: Biblical Exegesis, Feminist Theory, and the Laughter of Delight**

Peter D. Blair: **Congress's Own Think Tank: Learning from the Legacy of the Office of Technology Assessment (1973–1995)**

Daniel Tröhler: **Pestalozzi and the Educationalization of the World**

Geraldine Vaughan: **The 'Local' Irish in the West of Scotland, 1851–1921**

Matthew Feldman: **Ezra Pound's Fascist Propaganda, 1935–45**

Albert N. Link and John T. Scott: **Bending the Arc of Innovation: Public Support of R&D in Small, Entrepreneurial Firms**

Amir Idris: **Identity, Citizenship, and Violence in Two Sudans: Reimagining a Common Future**

Anshu Saxena Arora: **International Business Realisms: Globalizing Locally Responsive and Internationally Connected Business Disciplines**

G. Douglas Atkins: **T.S. Eliot and the Failure to Connect: Satire and Modern Misunderstandings**

Piero Formica: **Stories of Innovation for the Millennial Generation: The Lynceus Long View**

J. David Alvis and Jason R. Jividen: **Statesmanship and Progressive Reform: An Assessment of Herbert Croly's Abraham Lincoln**

David Munro: **A Guide to SME Financing**

Claudio Giachetti: **Competitive Dynamics in the Mobile Phone Industry**

R. Mark Isaac and Douglas A. Norton: **Just the Facts Ma'am: A Case Study of the Reversal of Corruption in the Los Angeles Police Department**

Huw Macartney: **The Debt Crisis and European Democratic Legitimacy**

Chiara Mio: **Towards a Sustainable University: The Ca' Foscari Experience**

Jordi Cat: **Maxwell, Sutton and the Birth of Color Photography: A Binocular Study**

Nevenko Bartulin: **Honorary Aryans: National–Racial Identity and Protected Jews in the Independent State of Croatia**

DOI: 10.1057/9781137343123

palgrave▶pivot

Fukushima and the Privatization of Risk

Majia Holmer Nadesan

Professor, Arizona State University, USA

DOI: 10.1057/9781137343123

First published 2013 by
PALGRAVE MACMILLAN

Palgrave Macmillan in the UK is an imprint of Macmillan Publishers Limited, registered in England, company number 785998, of Houndmills, Basingstoke, Hampshire RG21 6XS.

Palgrave Macmillan in the US is a division of St Martin's Press LLC, 175 Fifth Avenue, New York, NY 10010.

Palgrave Macmillan is the global academic imprint of the above companies and has companies and representatives throughout the world.

Palgrave® and Macmillan® are registered trademarks in the United States, the United Kingdom, Europe and other countries.

ISBN: 978-1-137-34313-0 EPUB
ISBN: 978-1-137-34312-3 PDF
ISBN: 978-1-137-34311-6 Hardback

A catalogue record for this book is available from the British Library.

A catalog record for this book is available from the Library of Congress.

www.palgrave.com/pivot

DOI: 10.1057/9781137343123

Fukushima and the Privatization of Risk is dedicated to the children of Fukushima and to the idea of a sustainable future for humanity.

DOI: 10.1057/9781137343123

Contents

DOI: 10.1057/9781137343123

DOI: 10.1057/9781137343123

Acknowledgements

Many people helped me learn about Fukushima. Thank you in particular to the two reviewers for this manuscript: Paul Dorfman and an anonymous reviewer. Thank you also Clyde Stagner, Robert Soltysik, Aaron Datesman, Paul Langley, Craig Daniels, Russell Smith, WhatAbout-TheKids, NoNukes, and the entire *Enenews* staff and community. Thank you Janie Briant for reading and editing my manuscript. Thank you Kamal and Ray for discussing scientific aspects and thank you to the rest of my family and friends for listening to me tell the story of *Fukushima and the Privatization of Risk*.

▶

DOI: 10.1057/9781137343123

1
Introduction to *Fukushima and the Privatization of Risk*

Abstract: *The public health risks from the Fukushima nuclear disaster will take decades to unfold and will be difficult to measure because of uncertainty about the extent of atmospheric and oceanic emissions and because of the challenges of mapping fallout patterns and bio-accumulation. The effect of uncertainty is that risk is privatized, or shifted away from Japanese industry and government, to impacted individuals in Japan and elsewhere.*

Keywords: Privatization of risk, Fukushima nuclear disaster, fallout, dose-effects models

Holmer Nadesan, Majia. *Fukushima and the Privatization of Risk*. Basingstoke: Palgrave Macmillan, 2013.
DOI: 10.1057/9781137343123.

Fukushima and the Privatization of Risk is a narrative of the Fukushima nuclear disaster that was caused by the great Honshu Quake of 11 March 2011. Three General Electric design reactors at the Fukushima Daiichi nuclear plant approximately 170 miles northeast of Tokyo were acknowledged by the operator, Tokyo Electric Power Corporation (TEPCO), to have had explosions and lose fuel containment in the days after the earthquake. The number of reactors involved, the scale of the explosions, and the reports of spent fuel pool fires raised international alarm about the potential for radiation contamination of northern Japan, the Pacific Ocean, and the western U.S. and Canada (including Hawaii and Alaska), which are directly downwind of Japan, by way of the jet stream. Yet, the crisis communications about the events at the plant by the Japanese government were reassuring in tone, for Japanese citizens, tending to de-emphasize risks posed by the events at the plant. The same tone was adopted by U.S. officials when asked about the potential for fallout to reach U.S. shores via the jet stream.

In the summer of 2012, the National Diet of Japan issued *The Official Report of the Fukushima Nuclear Accident Independent Investigation Commission*, chaired by Kiyoshi Kurokawa, a professor emeritus at the University of Tokyo. The report sharply chastised the management of the disaster by the Japanese government and TEPCO in the days immediately following the earthquake. The Diet report concludes that managing panic was prioritized over data-driven evacuation of citizens. The Diet report does not speculate on the potential effects of the disaster. However, concerns have been raised about the long-term effects on citizens in Fukushima, particularly for children especially given their vulnerabilities to ionizing radiation. Yet, cancers and other diseases caused by radiation typically take years, if not decades, to manifest. Therefore, the true risks for Fukushima residents and others exposed to Fukushima fallout will only be realized in the future, retrospectively, through epidemiological studies. These studies will be challenged by layers of uncertainty that complicate our understanding of the disaster. How much radiation was released into the air and ocean from March 2011 until today? How much radiation will bio-accumulate in human beings and what health effects can we expect? In a sense, the very uncertainty surrounding the scale of the disaster and the scope of its effects result in the privatization of risk.

The privatization of risk is a global social trend occurring in myriad ways as risk is shifted from organized entities – such as government and corporations – to private citizens. Risk is privatized when organized

DOI: 10.1057/9781137343123

institutions renegotiate social and economic contracts so that risk is shifted to individuals, who are made responsible for assuming costs. The U.S. sociologist Jacob Hacker was one of the first to describe how economic risk was being displaced from government and corporations to individuals and their families with the reduction of education, health, and welfare benefits.[1] The transfer of risk Hacker observed is a trend that can be found globally. Naomi Klein described a convergence of natural disaster and privatization of risk in *The Shock Doctrine*.[2] She has found the privatization of risk occurring in the response and aftermath of varied disasters ranging across the 2004 Asian Tsunami, 2005 Hurricane Katrina, and the Greek financial crisis of 2012. Across financial and environmental crises, the resulting privatization of risk promoted personal autonomy and action over social interventions, particularly when powerful opposing interests were involved.[3]

Another way of looking at the privatization of risk is to examine externalities. Externalities are indirect effects of production or consumption that affect individuals who are not the originators of the activity.[4] Industrial pollutants producing health risks for citizens illustrate externalities. Health externalities are largely absorbed by citizens through personal health spending and social and occupational impacts. Measurement of externalities can be challenging and tends to be retroactive in character. As explained by Kodama Tatsuhiko, Head of the Radioisotope Center at the University of Tokyo, when it comes to environmental produced disease, and especially radiation caused cancer, "epidemiological evidence is extremely hard [to establish], and in most cases, proof is impossible until all episodes finish running their course."[5] Tatsuhiko's point is that firm data on the relationship between disease and environmental causes are generally available only retrospectively. Thus, the affected present population typically absorbs the majority of the economic and social impacts. In this sense, externalities privatize risk.

This book examines the privatization of risk using both of these approaches. It examines how the economic and social costs of the Fukushima disaster are being shifted from TEPCO and the Japanese government to the impacted citizens of Japan and elsewhere. Those costs include loss of property value and, most importantly, risks to personal health. The Fukushima nuclear crisis has been labeled a "man-made disaster", yet the externalities of this event are likely going to be absorbed most by citizens in terms of personal impacts. This book focuses on the

DOI: 10.1057/9781137343123

health and personal impacts of the privatization of risk in the wake of this disaster at the Daiichi plant. Citizens are not without rights and those of Japan and elsewhere do have legal rights to compensation. However, efforts to attach financial value to probabilities of health impacts are complex and ultimately tentative.

It is also difficult to predict and quantify health impacts from this disaster for at least four important reasons: (1) the scale of emissions, though very great, is itself uncertain; (2) the extent of fallout and deposition patterns remain unclear; (3) the plant's status of "cold shutdown" does not preclude more significant releases of radiation; (4) the scientific literature on dose effects of ionizing radiation is contested and there exists considerable debate about the dominant models used to predict the probabilities of disease from exposure types and levels. Debates about the number of illnesses and fatalities from the Chernobyl accident, the Three Mile Island accident, and Cold War atmospheric testing continue even today. Uncertainty about emissions, fallout patterns, exposure levels, dose effects, and the lack of adequate control groups challenged efforts to monetize these past disasters and will challenge efforts now and in the future to quantify the effects of Fukushima.

It is difficult to predict and measure the health externalities of the disaster when so much uncertainty exists about the scale of the radiation emissions. Exact figures representing the scale and characteristics of emissions are not clear. The *Summary Report of Regional Specialized Metrological Center (RSMC) Beijing on Fukushima Nuclear Accident Emergency Response* submitted by RSMC Beijing in November 2011 claims that the radiation emitted from the plant in the first five days was "equal to that of the Chernobyl nuclear explosion," which burned for approximately ten days.[6] Kodama Tatsuhiko reported in July 2011 to a sub-committee of the Diet that radiation levels equivalent to 29.6 Hiroshima a-bombs were released, based on the analysis of the heat produced by the blasts.[7]

One element found in Fukushima fallout presenting particularly significant health risks is plutonium. Plutonium is produced as a by-product of the fissioning of uranium in nuclear reactors. How many uranium-based spent fuel rods were damaged by explosions and fire? Reactor 3 at the Fukushima Daiichi was running mixed-plutonium and uranium oxide (MOX) fuel at the time of the earthquake. It is unclear how many spent MOX rods were in unit 3 spent fuel storage pool and/or the common spent fuel pool. Although plutonium is an element, it is not found in nature and essentially all plutonium on earth was created through human activities.[8] It is highly radiotoxic. A single alpha emission from ingested plutonium can sever DNA. How much plutonium and uranium were released atmospherically in that reactor explosion? No full account has been provided, although plutonium from Japan's nuclear meltdowns has been detected as far away as Lithuania.[9]

Another radioactive element produced in vast quantity by the fissioning of uranium is cesium. Vast amounts of cesium were emitted from the Fukushima Daiichi explosions atmospherically in March 2011 and into the ocean nearly continuously because of ongoing leakages of radioactive water in the reactor units, which are located next to the Pacific. A stable isotope of cesium occurs naturally, but the radioactive forms, such as Cesium-137 and Cesium-134, emit beta particles (high speed electrons), and gamma rays (high frequency electromagnetic radiation), as they decay. Cesium is an analog of potassium so it is ingested by plants and animals, particularly when they are deficient in potassium. Radioactive isotopes of cesium therefore are highly likely to bio-accumulate and bio-magnify in plant and animal life.[10]

How much cesium and plutonium were released into the air and the sea by the Fukushima disaster? TEPCO's figures for atmospheric emissions are limited to the first months of the disaster and have been revised multiple times. Furthermore, TEPCO's figures are not consistent with some independent assessments[11] and have been challenged by former government officials within Japan.[12] Fallout maps of contamination in Japan are incomplete and may not incorporate hot spots. Use of salt water to cool the heated fuel rods in March 2011 may have increased the transportability of radioisotopes, further complicating understanding of the extent of releases.[13] Ocean contamination is even more difficult to map.

How much more radiation has been released over the last two years? The Japanese government reported in November 2011 that nuclear fission by-products were detected at Daiichi's unit 2 reactor, indicating ongoing nuclear chain reactions (or "criticalities") at the plant.[14] TEPCO acknowledged in July 2012 that the plant continued to emit radiation into the atmosphere, offering an estimate of emissions of 10 million Becquerels per hour.[15] The measurement "Becquerels" refers to the rate of disintegration of atoms. The plant has therefore been emitting measurable radiation into the atmosphere continuously since the first explosion in March 2011. Ocean contamination is also ongoing. Japanese and U.S. marine

DOI: 10.1057/9781137343123

scientists interviewed by *The Asahi Shimbun* in November 2012 reported suspicions that cesium leakages into the ocean continue unabated.[16]

Adding to uncertainty about emissions is the indeterminate risk of another very large atmospheric release. TEPCO officials declared "cold shutdown" in December 2011 despite detections of recent fission activities and evidence of ongoing steam and smoke emissions visible on the live-streaming and publicly available TEPCO and TBS-JNN webcams trained on the plant.[17] The Japanese paper *The Mainichi* ran an article attempting to reduce the ambiguity, "What Is a 'Cold Shutdown' at the Fukushima Nuclear Plant?" The article compared the typical technical use of the term cold shutdown with the Japanese government's use of the term for the state of the Fukushima Daiichi plant.[18] In the case of Daiichi, a designation of cold shutdown did not preclude to spontaneous fission events and ongoing radioactive decay at the plant.[19]

What health risks face citizens of Japan and elsewhere impacted by the dispersion of fallout through weather patterns and ocean currents? What levels of fallout pose threats to health? In January 2012, *The Asahi Shimbun* reported "Fukushima people eating more cesium but not in danger, says study."[20] Periodically spiking levels of Iodine-131, a fission product with an eight-day half-life, continued to be detected in sewage sludge in municipalities throughout Japan, including Tokyo.[21] The U.S. media also reported measurements of radiation contamination in Southern California seaweed and tuna published in scientific research.[22] What risks do detected contamination levels in the food chain pose for the people who are also subject to measurable amounts of Fukushima fallout in air and drinking water? Citizens are often not told the precise risks posed by increased radioisotopes of cesium, uranium, and plutonium in their environment, nor the assumptions upon which the risk models were built.

Granted, measuring health risks is challenging given inadequate information about the extent and distribution of actual fallout and limited measurements of its uptake in the environment. Nuclear fallout, in the form of radioactive elements such as uranium and cesium, does not disperse evenly in the atmosphere, but rather is transported by weather patterns and conditions through wind and precipitation. Radioisotopes in the ocean are distributed by currents and other oceanic conditions. Animals' absorptions of radioisotopes such as cesium-137 and strontium-90 distribute them still farther. Bio-magnification occurs as contamination increases across the food chain. Risks for people and the environment will emerge retroactive from the data collected in

DOI: 10.1057/9781137343123

longitudinal studies of fallout deposition, bio-accumulation, and inter-generational effects on fauna. Research from past nuclear disasters indicates that fallout bio-accumulates and bio-magnifies in the food chain across decades, although considerable variation exists depending upon the decay rate of the isotope and its chemical properties. Cesium-137 from the 1989 Chernobyl nuclear disaster, for example, continues to persist at high levels in wildlife in Belarus.[23]

The lack of clear data on emissions, fallout levels, and bio-accumulation complicate efforts to model risks for human populations. Already, con-flicting risk estimates have been reported. For example, *The Japan Times* in December 2012 reported the World Health Organization's (WHO's) statistical projections have been challenged publicly by Dr. Alex Rosen of the University Clinic Düsseldorf, also representing the International Physicians for the Prevention of Nuclear War.[24] The tendency for official estimates, such as the WHO's, to be lower than estimates offered by independent assessments means that the costs from any uncertainty in risk estimate are likely to be shifted to the citizens of Fukushima and elsewhere impacted by the fallout.

Furthermore, debate exists within the scientific community about the precise dose effects from radiation. Ionizing radiation is known to dam-age DNA bases through both direct and indirect effects, but many vari-ables mediate the quality and time-span of measurable effects, including the energy deposition of various forms of radiation and demographic variables of impacted populations, ranging from age to lifestyle and per-sonal susceptibilities.[25] Exposure variables are complex and include the pathway of exposure (e.g., internal or external), the number of exposures (including chronic exposure), and chemical mixtures that might exac-erbate effects.[26] Modeling dose effects is challenging and disagreement exists within the scientific community about the validity of standardized probability models, such as the risk model offered by International Commission on Radiological Protection (ICRP). Disagreement about dose effects is not a new phenomenon, but in this book will be traced back in time to conflicts that arose in the 1950s during atmospheric test-ing between geneticists and scientists employed by government nuclear power complexes, especially in the United States.

By 1927 the U.S. geneticist H. J. Muller had proven that relatively low levels of X-rays cause chromosomal mutations[27] and well-publicized incidences of radium poisoning raised international alarm about the risks posed by radioactive substances in the workplace and in consumer

DOI: 10.1057/9781137343123

products, resulting in the formation of international radiation protection committees, such as the ICRP in 1928. Yet, consensus was elusive about the precise dangers posed by different forms of ionizing radiation, particularly in the post-World War II era as nuclear testing and nuclear power development surged. For instance, the U.S. Atomic Energy Commission (AEC) insisted during atmospheric testing in the 1950s that all forms of radiation were equivalent to "sunshine" in their effects.[28] Scientists weighing in on the debate at the time were largely divided between physicists, who downplayed the biological effects, and geneticists, who were alarmed by chromosomal damage caused by relatively low levels of radiation and saw direct risks from the ingestion of radioisotopes. The 1956 *Biological Effects of Atomic Radiation: A Report to the Public from a Study by The National Academy of Sciences* (BEAR), which will be examined in detail in this book, illustrates the competing pressures by these divergent interests. Conflict about radiation safety persists into the present era, as a review and analysis of epidemiological and clinical research on radiation health effects will reveal.

Although precise calculations of risk are elusive, it is clear that people closest to the Daiichi plant in Japan are at the most risk because their exposure is the greatest. How much risk are they facing over time? The Japanese government has initiated some surveys and has installed some fallout monitors, but these provide incomplete data and results have not always been consistent with findings by citizens and scientists, especially of hot spots. The extent of food and water contamination is also unknown. Bio-accumulation and bio-magnification unfold across decades, especially for humans, who are near the top of the food chain. Uncertainty shifts the burden of risk to affected people.

In the spring of 2012 the evacuation zone around the plant was reduced and some displaced residents were encouraged to return, despite independent testing by Japanese citizens of high contamination in areas officially deemed as safe.[29] Japanese citizens receiving relief for their evacuation will no longer receive benefits after their homes have been declared safe to return to. This has meant that citizens are being forced to assume and shoulder the risks of living in contaminated areas.[30] Residents from Fukushima Prefecture have argued that they are being expected to live with much more radiation contamination and risk than the rest of the Japanese population. The true extent of contamination and the risks presented will not be mapped for generations, if ever.

DOI: 10.1057/9781137343123

Accordingly, *Fukushima and the Privatization of Risk* argues that risk has been shifted to citizens – privatized – by contextualizing the Fukushima disaster historically and in relation to the scientific and medical developments in our understandings of the health risks of ionizing radiation. It examines how risk has been privatized as Japanese citizens impacted by the disaster have been encouraged to return to areas that were highly contaminated by the disaster. It also examines efforts by government agencies and corporations to shift the externalities of the disaster to citizens through limited evacuations, bailouts, taxes, and other nuclear polices that transfer costs to citizens. In discussing these risk shifts this book raises concern about the privatization of risk in the wake of truly catastrophic events such as the Fukushima disaster. As observed by Graciela Chichilnisky, Chair of Columbia's Center for Risk Management: "We need better forms of social organization to face catastrophic risks today, particularly when the risks have been assumed by privatize citizens who lack the resources of most bureaucracies and corporations."[31]

In the wake of the disaster, Japan's Liberal Democratic Party (LDP) assumed power in December 2012 elections. The LDP embraces nuclear power in Japan despite seismic analyses that have found active faults under many plants. Why has nuclear power been pursued relentlessly despite the risks demonstrated by Fukushima, Chernobyl, Three Mile Island, among other nuclear disasters? The answer lies in the intimate connection between nuclear energy and nuclear weapons. Nuclear reactors not only afford energy for domestic consumption, but also provide nations with supplies and facilities necessary for production of nuclear weapons. In September 2012, Japan's Defense Chief Satoshi Morimoto asserted publicly that nuclear power plants pose a "deterrent" against foreign attacks.[32] The LDP subscribes strongly to this position.

Fukushima and the Privatization of Risk also explores the close historical coupling between nuclear weapons development and nuclear power in order to investigate a less-examined reason for the Japanese government's reluctance to halt all nuclear power despite post-March 11 findings that nuclear plants in Japan may reside on active faults. Rising tensions in Asia between Japan and China, particularly over territorial disputes, signals the potential for a rising new cold war.[33] Global and regional political tensions may play an under-recognized role in shaping the Japanese government's reluctance to close nuclear energy production in the nation, particularly at plants known to reside on active faults. In that respect, Japan's close relationship to the United States presently,

DOI: 10.1057/9781137343123

and in the post-World War period, also offers insight into the origins and management of the Fukushima crisis given several of the reactors at Fukushima Daiichi were designed by General Electric and the earliest units were built by a U.S. contractor. In many ways, the story of the evolution of the Fukushima disaster is also a story of the close nuclear-industrial relationships between the United States and Japan in the post-World War II era.

The book is organized into three separate parts, each of which can be read independently. Chapter 1 introduces the book and establishes its global environmental significance. Chapter 2 explains the development of the industrial-military nuclear complex in Japan and provides background on the Fukushima Daiichi plant. Chapter 3 addresses the Fukushima disaster and the crisis management efforts of the Japanese and U.S. governments. It also examines the empirical evidence of fallout and bio-contamination. Chapter 4 contextualizes the significance of the disaster in relation to the harmful effects of ionizing radiation. This chapter explores the politics inherent in the concept of a "permissible dose" and the historical and contemporary debates about measurement of biological effects. The significance of the Fukushima disaster is contextualized within new understandings of the biological effects of radiation on human health generally and the human genome more specifically. Chapter 5 concludes the book.

Notes

1 J. S. Hacker (May 2004) 'Privatizing Risk without Privatizing the Welfare State: The Hidden Politics of Social Policy Retrenchment in the United States', *American Political Science Review*, 98, 243–260.

2 N. Klein (2008) *The Shock Doctrine: The Rise of Disaster Capitalism* (New York: Picador).

3 See B. Rockhill's (2001) discussion of these characteristics of privatization processes in "The Privatization of Risk," *American Journal of Public Health*, 91, 365–368, p. 365.

4 J. J. Laffont (10 December 2012) "Externalities," in S. Durlauf and L. Blume (eds) *The New Palgrave Dictionary of Economics* 2nd edn (Basingstoke: Palgrave Macmillan, 2008), http://www.dictionaryofeconomics.com/article?id=pde2008_E000200>, date accessed 10 December 2012.

5 K. Tatsuhiko (8 August 2011) "Radiation Effects on Health: Protect the Children of Fukushima," translated by K. Selden, *The Asia Pacific Journal*, http://japanfocus.org/-Kodama-Tatsuhiko/3587, date accessed 9 August 2011.

DOI: 10.1057/9781137343123

6 World Metrological Organization (November 2011) "Summary Report of RSMC Beijing [Regional Specialized Meteorological Center] on Fukushima Nuclear Accident Emergency Response" CBS/CG-NERA/ Doc. 5.4 (27.10.2011), http://www.google.com/url?sa=t&rct=j&q=&esrc= s&source=web&cd=1&ved=0CDYQFjAA&url=http%3A%2F%2Fwww. wmo.int%2Fpages%2Fprog%2Fwww%2FDPFSERA%2FMeetings%2FCG-NERA_Vienna2011%2Fdocuments%2FDoc-5-4-China.doc&ei=8tnpUJTfFtPE 2QXZ5IHQAw&usg=AFQjCNEAY-JAKz38DrEHLefh1MGtyC4dqQ&bvm= bv.1355534169,d.b2U, p. 4, date accessed 3 November 2011.

7 Tatsuhiko, "Radiation Effects on Health."

8 Argonne National Laboratory (August 2005) "Plutonium," *Human Health Fact Sheet*, http://www.evs.anl.gov/pub/doc/Plutonium.pdf, date accessed 7 May 2012.

9 Detections of plutonium in Lithuania available here. G. Lujanienė, S. Byčenkienė, P. Povinec, M. Gera (27 December 2011) "Radionuclides from the Fukushima Accident in the Air over Lithuania: Measurement and Modeling Approaches," *Journal of Environmental Radioactivity*, 114, 71–80.

10 See Y-G Zhu and E. Smolders (2000) "Plant Uptake of Radiocaesium: A Review of Mechanisms, Regulation and Application," *Journal of Experimental Botany*, 51(351), 1635–1645.

11 A study challenging TEPCO's early estimates of radiation released: A. Stohl, P. Seibert, G. Wotawa, D. Arnold, J. F. Burkhart, S. Eckhardt, C. Tapia, A. Vargas, and T. J. Yasunari (2011) "Xenon-133 and Caesium-137 Releases into the Atmosphere from the Fukushima Daiichi Nuclear Power Plant: Determination of the Source Term, Atmospheric Dispersion, and Deposition," *Atmospheric Chemistry and Physics*, 12, 2313–2343. The French anti-nuclear organization AIPRI (Association Internationale pour la Protection contre les Rayons Ionisants [International Association for Protection against Ionizing Rays]) calculated 400.8 million toxic doses from xenon alone were released from Fukushima. AIPRI (4 November 2011) "Le Xenon 133 Très Faiblement Radiotoxique de Fukushima," http://aipri. blogspot.com/2011/11/le-xenon-133-tres-faiblement.html, date accessed 27 November 2011.

12 Former Minister for Internal Affairs Haraguchi Kazuhiro has alleged that radiation monitoring station data was actually three decimal places greater than the numbers released to the public. Cited in M. Penney (1 July 2011) "Nuclear Workers and Fukushima Residents at Risk: Japanese Cancer Expert on the Fukushima Situation," *The Asia Pacific Journal*, http://japanfocus.org/ events/view/100, date accessed 7 July 2011.

13 For research on the transportability of radioisotopes see C. Armstrong, M. Nyman, T. Shvareva, G. Sigmon, P. Burns, and A. Navrotsky (2012) "Uranyl Peroxide Enhanced Nuclear Fuel Corrosion in Seawater," *Proceedings of the National Academy of Sciences*, 109.6, 1874–1877.

DOI: 10.1057/9781137343123

14   M. Obe and S. Schroter (3 November 2011) "Damaged Japan Nuclear Reactor May Still Be Active," *The Wall Street Journal*, A11.

15   T. Sugimoto (24 July 2012) "After 500 Days, Fukushima No. 1 Plant Still Not Out of The Woods," *The Asahi Shimbun*, http://ajw.asahi.com/article/0311disaster/fukushima/AJ201207240087, date accessed 24 July 2012.

16   The marine scientists were Kenneth Buesseler of the US Woods Hole and Hideo Yamazaki, a marine biologist at Kinki University, whom were both quoted in the Associated Press article: K. Buesseler and H. Yamazaki (26 October 2012) "Cesium Levels in Fish off Fukushima Not Dropping," *The Asahi Shimbun*, http://ajw.asahi.com/article/0311disaster/fukushima/AJ201210260047, date accessed 26 October 2012.

17   T. Inajima and Y. Okada (2 November 2011) "TEPCO Detects Nuclear Fission at Damaged Fukushima Power Station," *Business Week*, http://www.businessweek.com/news/2011–11–01/TEPCO-detects-possible-nuclear-fission-at -fukushima-reactor.html, date accessed 4 November 2011.

18   "What Is a 'Cold Shutdown' at the Fukushima Nuclear Plant?" (17 December 2011) *The Mainichi Daily News*, http://mdn.mainichi.jp/perspectives/news/20111217p2a00m0na015000c.html, date accessed 17 December 2011.

19   Sugimoto "After 500 Days."

20   "Fukushima People Eating More Cesium But Not in Danger, Says Study" (19 January 2012), *The Asahi Shimbun*, http://ajw.asahi.com/article/0311disaster/fukushima/AJ201201190032, date accessed 19 January 2012.

21   Japanese municipal entities have been reporting concentrations of Iodine-131 in sewage sludge. For instance, Tokyo's report for contamination in sludge and incineration ash dated 6 December 2011 for many areas of Japan is available at www.gesui.metro.tokyo.jp/oshi/infn0579.htm. Gunma's report is available at http://www.pref.gunma.jp/cate_list/ct00005089.html. Increasing detections of Iodine-131, which has an eight-day half-life, indicate ongoing fission. C. Busby (27 December 2011) *Russia Today*, http://www.youtube.com/watch?v=1FouFAWV7uc, date accessed 30 December 2011.

22   D. J. Madigan, Z. Baumann, and N. S. Fisher (29 May 2012) "Pacific Bluefin Tuna Transport Fukushima-Derived Radionuclides from Japan to California," *Proceedings of the National Academy of Sciences*, http://www.pnas.org/content/early/2012/05/22/1204859109.full.pdf+html and "Study Finds Radioactive Fallout in California Kelp Beds" (5 April 2012), *Everything Long Beach*, http://www.everythinglongbeach.com/study-finds-radioactive-fallout-in-california-kelp-beds/, date accessed 6 April 2012.

23   I. Matusuo (28 March 2012) "Cesium Levels in Animals around Chernobyl Fail to Drop," *The Asahi Shimbun*, http://ajw.asahi.com/article/0311disaster/analysis/AJ201203280003, date accessed 28 March 2012.

DOI: 10.1057/9781137343123

24 "WHO Downplayed Health Effects of Nuclear Crisis on Fukushima Residents: German Physician" (16 December 2012), *Japan Times*, http://www.japantimes.co.jp/text/nn20121216a4.html, date accessed 16 December 2012.

25 E. Friedberg, G. Walker, W. Siede, R. Wood, R. Schultz, and T. Ellenberger (2006) *DNA Repair and Mutagenesis*, 2nd edn (Washington DC: ASM Press), p. 9.

26 A. O. Smith and J. S. Robert (2008) "Conceptual and Normative Dimensions of Toxicogenomics," in R. Sharp, G. Marchant, and J. Grodsky (eds), *Genomics and Environmental Regulation: Science, Ethics, and Law* (Baltimore: John Hopkins), p. 230.

27 H. J. Muller (1927) "Artificial Transmutation of the Gene," *Science,* **46**, 84–87.

28 R. L. Miller (1986) *Under the Cloud: The Decades of Nuclear Testing* (New York: The Free Press), p. 203.

29 See "Japanese Town Split by Radiation Evacuation Zone" (8 March 2012), *The Journal of Turkish Weekly*, http://www.turkishweekly.net/news/132185/japanese-town-split-by-radiation-evacuation-zone.html, date accessed 12 June 2012.

30 As documented here: A. Froggatt, D. McNeill, S. Thomas and R. Teul (February 2013) "Fukushima Fallout: Nuclear Business Makes People Pay and Suffer" (Amsterdam: Greenpeace), http://www.greenpeace.org/international/Global/international/publications/nuclear/2013/FukushimaFallout.pdf, date accessed 28 February 2013.

31 G. Chichilnisky (7 June 2006) "Catastrophic Risks: The Need for New Tools, Financial Instruments and Institutions," *The Privatization of Risk*, http://privatizationofrisk.ssrc.org/Chichilnisky/, date accessed 7 November 2012.

32 "Japan Sees Nuclear Power Plants as Powerful 'Deterrent' against Foreign Attacks" (6 September 2012) *Newstrack India*, http://newstrackindia.com/newsdetails/2012/09/06/231-Japan-sees-nuclear-power-plants-as-powerful-deterrent-against-foreign-attacks.html, date accessed 9 February 2013.

33 See M. Klare (6 December 2011) "Tomgram: A New Cold War in Asia?" *Tomdispatch*, http://www.tomdispatch.com/blog/175476/, date accessed 12 December 2011.

DOI: 10.1057/9781137343123

2
Why Nuclear Power

Abstract: *Nuclear energy and nuclear weapons have been historically connected in Japan and elsewhere. Japan's nuclear energy program, particularly, its breeder reactor program and used fuel reprocessing, has been directly linked to its national security. This chapter explores how nuclear energy became an important foundation of Japan's national security and considers the implications given Japan's earthquake and tsunami activity.*

Keywords: Uranium enrichment, breeder reactors, history of Japan's nuclear energy industry, Matsutaro Shoriki, Atomic Energy Basic Law of 1955, the Aerospace Law of 2008, nuclear deterrence, and national security

Holmer Nadesan, Majia. *Fukushima and the Privatization of Risk*. Basingstoke: Palgrave Macmillan, 2013.
DOI: 10.1057/9781137343123.

DOI: 10.1057/9781137343123

Nuclear power has from its beginnings been tied closely to nuclear weapons production. Manhattan scientists' success during World War II in unleashing vast power through fission – a process of deconstructing atoms – suggested the possibility of harnessing this power for peaceful energy production. The financial costs and practical challenges of harnessing nuclear energy were discounted by enthusiastic supporters in the post-war context who saw in it a strategy for simultaneously ensuring energy requirements for industrializing societies and enriched uranium and plutonium for nuclear weapons production,[1] which were believed capable of keeping peace by deterring unwinnable war.[2] Thus, despite engineering challenges, prohibitive costs, and public discomfort about radiation, the major industrial powers launched their nuclear energy programs. The United States led the way and played a vital role in establishing national and international agencies that would promote nuclear power in the Western world. Great Britain (UK), France, and the Soviet Union followed suit. Japan, locked in a post-World War relationship with the United States, ultimately adopted nuclear energy for strategic energy and, perhaps, for military purposes as well. Many of its earliest reactors were built by U.S. companies. This chapter briefs the development of nuclear power as part of the early "Atoms for Peace" program heralded by Eisenhower but embraced by many Cold War nuclear powers. The chapter then sketches development of Japan's nuclear industry in the context of a powerful international nuclear-industrial complex.

One theme developed in this chapter is that governments desired membership in the "nuclear club" of nuclear capable nations for both energy and military -security imperatives. Nuclear energy didn't simply promise energy independence. It also enabled access to the uranium refinement capabilities necessary for building nuclear weapons that promised deterrent force. As David Elliot notes, "To date, all the known nuclear weapons in the world have been produced by states (Israel apart) with civil nuclear technology; the technologies are inevitably intertwined, often making it hard to detect which option is being emphasized."[3]

Proliferation of nuclear weapons in Asia has been driven by "a push for national security," as explained by Paul Bracken in "The Second Nuclear Age."[4] Nuclear energy programs may be seen by nations as posing a degree of deterrent power even in the absence of outright weapons development. Nations signing the Treaty on the Non-Proliferation of Nuclear Weapons do not violate the terms of the treaty by stockpiling plutonium officially designated for use in breeder nuclear energy facilities. Yet, those stockpiles

DOI: 10.1057/9781137343123

may signal to others nuclear weapons capabilities, thereby functioning as a kind of deterrent force in the absence of actual weapons development.

The chapter begins by sketching the birth of the atomic age and the establishment of nuclear power for domestic energy in the context of concerns about global nuclear weapons proliferation. It then focuses specifically on the development of Japan's nuclear energy program despite widespread domestic fears about nuclear power caused by World War II bombings and, later, by atmospheric testing.

Nuclear energy and Atoms for Peace

The atomic age truly was materialized in war with the Manhattan Project, but the possibilities for peace were loudly heralded in the post-World War II context. Nuclear power would simultaneously solve problem of carbon-based energy limits and enrich the nuclear power industries – especially the engineers and contractors – primarily of the United States, United Kingdom, France, Canada, Soviet Union, and later Japan. The prospects for limitless peace and prosperity were loudly triumphed. Indeed, the 22 December 1945 issue of *Science News Letters* proudly declared "Atomic Power Leads" as the year's most significant scientific advancement given its "world shaking consequences."[5] The Japanese cities of Hiroshima and Nagasaki experienced those world shaking consequences first hand with the deployments of the "Little Boy" uranium weapon on Hiroshima on 6 August 1945 and the "Fat Man" plutonium-based bomb over Nagasaki on 9 August. However, the article in *Science News Letters* emphasized the medical benefits of newly discovered radiological isotopes over the destructive power of fallout. This tendency to emphasize purported benefits of all things nuclear by scientific and government authorities was a strategy to sell the world on the benefits of nuclear power.

The idea of using nuclear energy for civilian energy purposes was legitimized publicly in an address by President Dwight D. Eisenhower to the 470th Plenary Meeting of the United Nations General Assembly on 8 December 1953. This speech has come to be known as "Atoms for Peace." The text is a masterpiece of inversion, transforming the horrors of nuclear weapons into the productive, peaceful promise of nuclear energy:

> The United States would seek more than the mere reduction or elimina-
> tion of atomic materials for military purposes. It is not enough to take
> this weapon out of the hands of the soldiers. It must be put into the hands

DOI: 10.1057/9781137343123

of those who will know how to strip its military casing and adapt it to the arts of peace.

The United States knows that if the fearful trend of atomic military build-up can be reversed, this greatest of destructive forces can be developed into a great boon, for the benefit of all mankind. The United States knows that peaceful power from atomic energy is no dream of the future. The capability, already proved, is here today.[6]

Eisenhower outlined the U.S.'s leadership role in this transformation: "The United States would be more than willing – it would be proud to take up with others 'principally involved' the development of plans whereby such peaceful use of atomic energy would be expedited." He tasked the United Nations with the creation of an international atomic energy agency responsible for monitoring and governing a stockpile of uranium and fissionable materials that could be employed for the "peaceful" development of nuclear energy. Nuclear energy was being heralded as provider of perpetual peace by eliminating energy resource scarcity.[7]

The international agency set up to help oversee and promote the global nuclear industry was the International Atomic Energy Agency (IAEA). It played a historically important role in promoting through research and training nuclear power for Western countries and their nuclear industries.[8] It set up a Department of Technical Assistance and a Joint Division with the U.N. Food and Agricultural Organization (FAO). The IAEA also inaugurated the Internal Centre for Theoretical Physics, which trained scientists from the developing countries and supported their research. Today, it organizes and promotes international conferences on the "peaceful uses of nuclear energy," the first of which was held in August 1955. The IAEA endows research at institutes through grants, a practice that began in 1960 and continues today.[9]

Atoms for Peace and the IAEA promoted peaceful uses of nuclear in reactors built to create energy, but atomic knowledge and technology were closely tied to nuclear weapons production. The nuclear fission of the Uranium-235 based Hiroshima bomb is similar to the fissioning of Uranium-235 in a commercial nuclear energy reactor, although the density of the atoms is greater in bomb materials. Uranium must be highly enriched for weapons by increasing the proportion of Uranium-235.

It was clear that the spread of commercial nuclear energy would increase the risks of nuclear weapons proliferation. Efforts to control proliferation became an international agenda, particularly during the Cold War. At a practical level it was believed that proliferation could be

DOI: 10.1057/9781137343123

limited by promoting slower operating reactors for commercial power. For example, the U.S.-engineered light-water reactors promoted by Eisenhower's Atoms for Peace were not well suited for nuclear weapons production because they use relatively "low-enriched" Uranium-235 and Uranium-238 and consume more fissile material than they produce.[10] However, it was recognized that the uranium and plutonium isotopes present in spent nuclear fuel could be extracted by "reprocessing" and then enriched. In effect, weapons grade fissile material could be created from the waste of nuclear reactors used for civilian energy production.

Experimental "breeder" reactor programs provided a rationale for fuel reprocessing, while simultaneously enabling production of weapons grade plutonium. Fast-neutron, breeder reactors run on enriched fuel containing greater concentrations of fissile radioisotopes, such as U-235. Breeders, unlike boiling water reactors, also produce more fissile material than they consume. France, the United Kingdom, United States, and Japan all pursued commercially aimed breeder programs, especially in the 1950s, because they promised to close the fuel cycle, reducing dependency upon new sources of uranium through reclamation and redeployment of actinide waste.[11] Spent fuel reprocessing was launched in countries hoping to deploy breeder reactor programs.[12] A successful breeder program promised to bolster national security by producing energy, reducing nuclear waste, and ensuring access to enriched uranium and weapons grade plutonium. Breeder reactor programs, however, presented two important problems.

The first problem centered on the security issues surrounding proliferation of weapons grade actinides, especially plutonium, officially designated for breeder reactor programs. A nation could have on hand the resources needed for nuclear weapons while remaining officially committed to non-proliferation. Ambiguity of intent served strategic purposes. Plutonium was the ultimate Cold-War weapons material and global powers signaled prowess with their plutonium stockpiles, along with the missile technology required for delivery. For example, the Argonne National Laboratory reports that the United States stockpiled about 110,000 kilograms (kg) of plutonium between 1944 and 1994, and about 100,000 kg remains in inventory.[13] Breeder reactor programs therefore offered nations nuanced forms of security, while simultaneously increasing global insecurity.

The second problem with breeder reactors is that they are quite risky to operate. All types of nuclear reactors can suffer from loss of cooling

DOI: 10.1057/9781137343123

accidents and from "reactivity excursion" where control of the reactor core is lost, resulting in a runaway nuclear reaction.[14] Breeder reactors are particularly prone to these types of accidents because they use sodium (rather than water) to mediate reactions, which promotes a faster reaction. Sodium burns if exposed to air and reacts violently with water. Preventing contamination of the sodium by water or air has proven difficult.[15] So, many commercially aimed breeder reactor programs around the world were halted because their perceived risks outweighed their benefits in a context of affordable uranium and global plutonium stockpiles. Japan alone pursued a "commercial" breeder reactor program, until it was closed in early 2012.

Cold-War plutonium stockpiles posed significant security risks that became more obvious with the collapse of the Soviet Union. Subsequent efforts to draw down plutonium stockpiles focused on "recycling" the plutonium by blending it with uranium, producing MOX fuel that could be run in the "slower" commercial reactors that ultimately dominated the nuclear energy market. The risks of running MOX fuel in commercial reactors built primarily in the 1960s and 1970s are subject to debate, although will not be rehearsed here.

By global standards, Japan has a relatively extensive nuclear complex. It has a vast network of commercial nuclear power plants, and it has uranium-reprocessing capabilities at Tokai. It has two established breeder reactors : Jōyō reactor, which began operation in 1977, and the Monju reactor, with troubled beginnings in 1994. Japan has vast nuclear processing and MOX production capabilities at the Rokkasho plant. Japan's extensive nuclear capabilities are remarkable given strong anti-nuclear sentiments in the country after World War II. What follows is a description of how Japan's nuclear complex came to be.

Japan joins the nuclear club

Energy independence has been a long-term goal for Japan.[16] Nuclear energy promised energy autonomy and signaled Japan's deterrent capabilities. As *The Asahi Shimbun* notes in a 2012 editorial, "In both Japanese and English, the term 'national security' also means 'national defense'."[17] National defense has itself been constructed within a military frame.[18] In essence, Japanese leaders have regarded nuclear energy as promoting multiple forms of security.

DOI: 10.1057/9781137343123

Historical development of nuclear power in Japan was closely tied to the U.S. and U.K. nuclear industry and to U.S. government's efforts at nuclear promotion. Atoms for Peace facilitated the sale of American, British, and Canadian reactors to Japan. However, selling the Japanese people on nuclear power after the bombing of Hiroshima and Nagasaki took some work and the accidental irradiation of Japanese fishermen in the Bikini Atoll in 1954 added to Japanese citizens' distrust of nuclear energy. Many narratives can be told about development of support for nuclear energy in Japan. This section focuses on how a single Japanese citizen used his influence to cultivate acceptance of nuclear energy in one of the world's most geologically active nations. The story of Matsutaro Shoriki's influence over Japan's nuclear development follows.

In 2012, Tetsuo Arima, a researcher at Waseda University in Tokyo, disclosed contents of declassified CIA documents he found in the U.S. National Archives. The documents describe how Matsutaro Shoriki worked with the CIA to propagandize in favor of nuclear power using his position as head of *The Yomiuri Shimbun:*

> Mr. Shoriki, backed by the CIA, used his influence to publish articles in the Yomiuri that extolled the virtues of nuclear power, according to the documents found by Mr. Arima. Keen on remilitarizing Japan, Mr. Shoriki endorsed nuclear power in hopes its development would one day arm the country with the ability to make its own nuclear weapons, according to Mr. Arima. Mr. Shoriki's behind-the-scenes push created a chain reaction in other media that eventually changed public opinion.[19]

Shoriki is attributed with producing a shift in support for nuclear energy using his strategic influence of the media. Indeed, *The Economist* refers to him as the Japan's Citizen Kane.[20]

Matsutaro Shoriki acquired *The Yomiuri Shimbun* in the 1920s, when it was left in orientation. According to *The Economist*, Shoriki "turned it into a scrappy, sensational pugilist for right-wing politics." Cloaked in "public interest," the paper also promoted "gory sensationalism" to attract viewers, including American baseball, which Shoriki thought would interest mass audiences. Shoriki's stories and editorials in *The Yomiuri* publicized his viewpoints, helping him achieve a legislative seat in Japan's Diet on a pro-nuclear platform. He also founded the first commercial television station in Japan, Nippon Television Network Corporation. He used his influence to help forge the Liberal Democratic Party (LDP), founded in 1955, that "ruled Japan for almost all of the next 55 years," as described

DOI: 10.1057/9781137343123

in *The Economist*. The party's desire for nuclear power was because it was perceived as fulfilling two security needs: the need for energy and the need for the capability of a nuclear deterrent. Article 9 of Japan's Constitution prohibits a national act of war. Nuclear power would allow Japan to meet the terms of the constitution, while having on hand the materials necessary for creating nuclear weapon, which are regarded in some international contexts as the ultimate deterrent.

The Atomic Energy Basic Law was passed in 1955, the same year the LDP was formed. The law allowed for use of nuclear power for energy and created the Japanese Atomic Energy Commission (AEC) and the Japan Atomic Energy Research Institute. It dictated control over fissile materials, measures for patented inventions, and radiation protections. Article 21 of the law dictated compensation for nuclear accidents, although the law has been criticized for not specifying level of governmental responsibility. The year this law was passed, Shoriki invited John Jay Hopkins of General Dynamics and Laurence Hafstad of Chase Manhattan to lecture on atomic energy.[21] Shoriki encouraged Japan's Atomic Energy Commission to import nuclear technology from the United States and Britain. He dismissed concerns about safety from within the Japanese scientific community while pushing forward breeder technologies.[22] Shoriki played a vital role in forging public acceptance for nuclear power and by linking it to energy security publicly while bringing Japan into the nuclear club.

The nuclear energy industry grew quickly into a powerful complex. Japan's electrical companies have regional monopolies and are backed by the institutional power of Japan's Ministry of Economy, Trade, and Industry (METI). Japan's Nuclear and Industrial Safety Agency (NISA), which is under METI authority, both regulated and promoted nuclear power until a new "independent" agency, the Nuclear Regulation Authority (NRA) was created in September of 2012. Adding to the electrical companies' power are networks of influence cultivated by industry grants and personal honorariums. Cultivated networks of influential actors helped shape public opinion at national and regional levels. They have been active over the years in pushing municipalities to accept nuclear facilities. Critics argue that the utilities tendency to prioritize profit over safety, coupled with the unwillingness of Japan's regulatory system to plan for catastrophic conditions, were instrumental in creating the conditions of possibility for the Fukushima disaster.[23] Japan's forays into breeder reactors and reprocessing at Tokai and other locations

DOI: 10.1057/9781137343123

proceeded unchecked by public scrutiny in the context of this nuclear complex.

Reactors that reprocess nuclear fuel and/or that operate at higher temperatures using plutonium infused fuel have historically posed special engineering challenges, as discussed above. Japan struggled for years to develop a viable breeder reactor energy program that reduced nuclear waste and dependency upon uranium providers by exploiting the entire nuclear fuel cycle.[24] In 1967, the Japanese Atomic Energy Commission's (JAEC) first "Long Term Plan" promoted fast-breeder reactors as the mainstream for Japan's nuclear power future.[25] In 1988, *Physics Today* ran an article titled "Japan's Nuclear Program Stresses Breeders, Plutonium, and Safeguards."[26]

As of early 2012, Japan calculated that it had invested $12 billion in its experimental "Monju" sodium-cooled, fast-breeder reactor in Fukui Prefecture.[27] Designed to operate on plutonium from reprocessed, spent reactor fuel, Monju has been beset with problems since its construction began in 1986. The reactor began operation in 1994, but was soon shut down because of a major fire caused by a sodium leak in 1995.[28] The operator attempted to hide the incident by having workers alter their reports and through the creation of a strategically truncated video of the accident.[29] Operations resumed in 2010, but another malfunction occurred.

The death knell of the fast-breeder program occurred in a 23 February 2012 review by the Japan Atomic Energy Commission, which concluded that technological considerations prevented the program from being a realistic option.[30] By this time Japan had vast stockpiles of plutonium, stored domestically and abroad.[31] At the time of the Fukushima disaster, Japan had an inventory of more than 46 tons (8.7 Tons in Japan, approximately 37 tons in Europe) of separated plutonium.[32] (46 tons of plutonium equals to 41,730 kilograms.) Joseph Trento claims Japan's inventory of plutonium is actually 70 tons.[33] It was recognized that efforts would need to be made to draw down these plutonium stockpiles. The commission recommended that some of it be recycled into MOX fuel that could be used in adapted boiling water reactors.

Despite its interest in developing a successful breeder program, Japan's biggest utilities in the early 1960s, Tokyo Electric and Kansai Electric, had purchased American light water designs from General Electric and Westinghouse.[34] Tokyo Electric Power Company, formed in 1951, ordered its first boiling water reactor in 1966 from General Electric. During this

DOI: 10.1057/9781137343123

period, Japan's government offered special depreciation allowances and tax cuts to spur new orders and construction of nuclear power plants.

The Fukushima Daiichi reactor one was TEPCO's first boiling water nuclear reactor.[35] The earliest reactors at Daiichi were built in the 1960s by Ebasco, an American general contractor that no longer exists. Reactors 1 through 6 at the site were based on General Electric designs and reactors 1 through 5 relied on Mark I type containment structures. Retroactively, it is clear that the plant was not well-engineered for the site's geological risks. Kiyoshi Kishi, a former TEPCO executive heading TEPCO's nuclear plant engineering, was interviewed by *The Wall Street Journal* about the lack of tsunami precautions at the plant. Kishi was quoted as stating that at the time the plant was built, a threat posed by a large tsunami at the site was considered "impossible."[36] Later, some precautions were taken to protect the plant against a tsunami with a height of 18.8 feet. The tsunami that hit the plant on 11 March was over twice that height. TEPCO engineers interviewed by *The Wall Street Journal* also reported that the venting systems in reactors 1 through 5 were very inefficient. Flooding of the generators and the poor ventilations systems are cited as the causes of the meltdowns and explosions at the Daiichi units 1 through 4. The four reactors at the Fukushima Daini complex and building 6 at the Daiichi complex used General Electric's Mark II system and were purportedly tailored more specifically to meet Japan's earthquake and tsunami risks.[37] These reactor buildings were reported in this article as having shut down safely, although contradictory evidence exists about their safe shutdown that will be discussed presently.[38]

Japan's lax safety record is not the sole explanation for the Fukushima disaster. Two engineers at General Electric resigned in 1975 after concluding that the nuclear reactor designs for the Mark I reactors (built at Fukushima) were fundamentally flawed and dangerous. Boiling water reactors operate with intense pressure and the engineers felt that the design specifications were insufficient for handling pressures that would result from a loss of cooling accident. One of the engineers, Dale G. Bridenbaugh, explained the General Electric engineers' concerns in a recent interview with ABC: "The problems we identified in 1975 were that, in doing the design of the containment, they did not take into account the dynamic loads that could be experienced with a loss of coolant... The impact loads the containment would receive by this very rapid release of energy could tear the containment apart and create an uncontrolled release."[39]

DOI: 10.1057/9781137343123

That being said, it is notable that TEPCO's nuclear plants have been plagued with scandals. In March 1997 a small explosion and radiation release occurred at the Dōnen nuclear reprocessing plant. In 1999, the Jōyō fast-breeder uranium-reprocessing reactor at Tokai-mura (Ibaraki Prefecture) had an uncontrolled nuclear chain reaction that killed two employees and released radioactive emissions.[40] Reforms ensued. The Japanese Nuclear and Industrial Safety Agency was established in 2001 in response to central government reforms. At that time, a "Roundtable Committee on Fast Breeder Reactors was set up" to create new policies. The recommendation was to maintain the program, but to adopt a more pragmatic approach that regarded the program as an option, as opposed to an ultimate goal.[41]

Reforms during the early 2000s unearthed problems at commercial power plants in Japan. In 2002, TEPCO's president, vice president, and chairman stepped down after the utility acknowledged that it failed to report accurately cracks at its nuclear reactors in the 1980s and 1990s.[42] TEPCO was suspected of falsifying 29 cases of safety repair records. The Japanese NISA claimed that up to eight reactors could be operating with unfixed cracks, "though the cracks don't pose an immediate threat." In 2006, TEPCO was found to have falsified coolant water temperatures at the Fukushima Daiichi plant in 1985 and 1988.[43] The falsified records were used during a 2005 inspection. In the wake of these scandals, TEPCO revealed that an uncontrolled chain reaction had occurred in unit 3 at Fukushima Daiichi when fuel rods fell into the reactor.[44] TEPCO also acknowledged that it had falsified records of safety tests on unit 1's containment vessel that occurred during 1991–1992.[45] In 2010, unit 2 reactor stopped automatically after problems with a generator resulted in a steep drop in the water level inside the reactor by about 1.8 meters.

Problems continued. In July 2007, TEPCO's Kashiwazaki Kariwa nuclear power plant in Niigata Prefecture was damaged in a 6.8 magnitude earthquake.[46] TEPCO claimed no radiation was released, but later admitted radiation had vented and that radioactive water spilled into the Sea of Japan.[47] However, as with other countries experiencing nuclear contamination accidents, these incidences did not deter Japanese utilities or architects of nuclear power.

Japan's nuclear utilities and engineering companies are powerfully entrenched in Japan's economic and political spheres.[48] Indeed, despite domestic problems, Japan's government hopes to promote its nuclear industry abroad. For example, in August 2011, Japan's Ministry of

DOI: 10.1057/9781137343123

Economy, Trade and Industry visited Vietnam in order to promote sales of nuclear plants, anticipating that Japan will be contracted to build that nation's second nuclear plant. In June 2012, Hitachi announced that it plans to double its nuclear power sales and post-Fukushima disaster work.[49]

Japan's December 2012 election ushered in a majority for the conservative LDP, resulting in a more pro-nuclear and militant group of legislators. Shinzo Abe, the new prime minister, immediately called for restarting nuclear reactors and Japan's nuclear reprocessing idled after the March 2011 earthquake.[50] Japan's NRA backed restarts, although insisting on extensive geological and safety inspections. Nuclear energy was prioritized over the myriad economic and social risks caused by the Fukushima disaster.

Japan and the security of nuclear deterrence

Nuclear weapons were historically regarded as offering deterrent force because of the weapons' genocidal effects. There is considerable debate about whether or not Japan views its nuclear power program in terms of military security. In particular, debate exists over the role of Japan's reprocessing facilities and breeder reactors. Japan has a unique status as the only nonnuclear (weapons) country in the world that openly reprocesses its nuclear fuel.[51] Shoriki's LDP was, and remains, highly nationalistic. Did Japan pursue nuclear enrichment and plutonium stockpiling to signify nuclear weapons' capabilities?

Critics have questioned the purpose of Japan's plutonium policies given the element's hazards. In 1990, Junzaburo Takahi, a scientist with Japan's Citizens' Nuclear Information Center, and Baku Nishio, a staff member of that organization, described in *The Bulletin of the Atomic Scientists* Japan's "fake plutonium shortage." They also critiqued its plan to ship to Japan plutonium extracted in France and Britain at an estimated cost of 20 billion yen.[52] Japan risked accident, terrorism, and international criticism for pursuing plutonium stockpiles.

In 2008 Japan passed the Aerospace Law of 2008, which included a provision allowing development of space technology in relation to its "contribution to national security."[53] Japan's entry into this sector meant it would be working on missile technology capable of delivering nuclear weapons.[54] In 2011 Japan lifted its prohibition

DOI: 10.1057/9781137343123

against producing advanced weapons for export.[55] That same year Japan purchased 42 of Lockheed Martin Corporation's F-35 Lightning II Joint Strike Fighter planes to replace its Air Self Defense Force's 1960s-era F-4 jets.[56] Japan has most, if not all, of the capacities of a nuclear armed nation while still enjoying the overt protection of the U.S. nuclear umbrella.

Japan and the United States have reciprocal defense agreements. Many in Japan are uncomfortable with relying on the U.S. "nuclear umbrella," as it has come to be called. Japan's more pacifist anti-nuclear groups *and* its more hawk-like nationalists all take issue with the U.S. nuclear umbrella, albeit for very different reasons since the doves want to abolish all nuclear while the hawks want to formally institutionalize Japan's own nuclear deterrent capabilities. Until recently, Japan's leadership was content to rely formally on the United States for deterrence power. In 2010, Prime Minister Naoto Kan reaffirmed the nuclear deterrence power implicit in US-Japan defense agreements, despite the pleas of Hiroshima Mayor Akiba to forego nuclear protection.[57] At this time, Kan also reiterated Japan's adherence to the three nonnuclear principles against production, possession, and introduction of nuclear weapons in Japan, but would not support or sign legislation that would make the principles law.

Japan's status as nuclear weapons-capable is loudly broadcast through its uranium reprocessing and enrichment capabilities, plutonium stockpiles, and advanced aeronautical capabilities. For this reason, eyebrows were raised when it was reported that nuclear industry officials and scientists close to the industry decided in a secret meeting held in May 2012 to resume fuel reprocessing when all nuclear reactors in the country had been idled.[58] *The Mainichi* decried the secrecy, demanding an investigation.[59] Why was secrecy involved? Why did Japan need to reprocess, or enrich, more uranium?

The answer seemed to be that reprocessing is seen by the LDP as vital for Japan's national security. Indeed, LDP members and Japan's nuclear agency acted surreptitiously in 2012 to link reprocessing with national security. *The Asahi Shimbun* explained in an editorial:

> A revision to the Atomic Energy Basic Law adding an appendix stating that nuclear power should "contribute to national security" has passed the Diet. Those words, which could provoke suspicions that Japan is planning to develop nuclear weapons, should be deleted in the next Diet session. Nuclear law's "national security" clause must be dropped.[60]

DOI: 10.1057/9781137343123

The Mainichi speculated that the clause was designed to save the Rokkasho plant after the breeder reactor program closure and shutdown of Japan's commercial nuclear energy reactors:

> "It probably comes down to the Rokkasho Reprocessing Plant," said a bureaucrat with whom I've been acquainted for years. "If the country moves toward the abandonment of nuclear power, that facility will lose meaning. If it is legally granted legitimacy as a facility for the military use of nuclear materials, then it can continue to exist. I believe that there were LDP lawmakers who thought of that, and bureaucrats who supported them."[61]

The Mainichi described the clause as allowing "the possibility of nuclear armament open to interpretation,"[62] and called for its deletion:

> The amendment has fueled speculations about its true aim. Some wonder whether the interpretation of the clause could be stretched to open the way for nuclear weapons development. Others question whether the clause is aimed at underscoring the effectiveness of the development and use of atomic power for nuclear power plants and other purposes.[63]

Japan's energy security and military security were officially joined in September 2012 when Japan's Minister of Defense, Satoshi Morimoto, asserted that "nuclear plants give us deterrent force."[64] The LDP aggressively promoted this stance after taking office in 2013.

How realistic are concerns that reprocessing is used for producing nuclear weapons grade isotopes? Some claim that the plutonium processed from spent fuel is inadequate for weapons production. However, others disagree.[65] Piers Williamson, summarizing speeches delivered on 31 May 2012 by Professors Frank von Hippel (Princeton University) and Gordon MacKerron (University of Sussex), noted that Japan's stockpile of plutonium would enable production of 5,000 nuclear warheads.[66] Williamson explained that although Japan (purportedly) does not currently have a nuclear weapons program, it could easily produce one given the nation's technological sophistication and its plutonium stockpiles and that Japan's persistence in reprocessing is counter to international trends. Von Hippel commented in a November 2012 *New York Times* editorial with Masafumi Takumbo that "There is a real credibility problem here," especially with respect to the Rokkasho plant facilities.[67]

The LDP announced in January 2013 that it would continue the policy of fuel reprocessing,[68] despite warnings in December 2012 by two professors of geomorphology at Tokyo University that a 100 kilometer fault running directly under this plant was likely active, and could produce

DOI: 10.1057/9781137343123

an 8-magnitude quake.[69] Reprocessing was too closely linked to national security to end, particularly in the political context of rising territorial disputes with China.

At the beginning of 2013, more warlike rhetoric prevailed in LDP political discourse. *The Mainichi's* survey results indicated strong support among new legislators for eliminating the "war-renouncing" Article 9 of Japan's Constitution: "About 72 percent of 473 newly elected House of Representative lawmakers support the idea of revising war-renouncing Article 9 of the Constitution and 78 percent of the legislators say the government should change its constitutional interpretation that currently forbids Japan from exercising the right of collective self-defense."[70] *The Mainichi* concluded that 90 percent of the LDP legislators favor revising Article 9 of the Constitution. Rising geopolitical tensions with China no doubt contributed to this more aggressive stance, as illustrated by Japan's accusation earlier in February 2013 that China threatened its forces.[71] It appears that nuclear weapons capabilities remain integral to Japanese state security.

Nuclear and the privatization of risk

Japan's leadership, following the lead of other Western nations, has seen nuclear as fulfilling two national needs: energy and security. Japan's nuclear power industry has long been understood as posing deterrent force by demonstrating the nation's nuclear capabilities. The 2008 Aerospace Law and the recent June 2012 amendment to Japan's Atomic Energy Basic Law formally link nuclear energy generally and reprocessing specifically to national security through the nuclear deterrence power demonstrated by nuclear capabilities. The Rokkasho reprocessing plant, believed to sit upon an active fault, illustrates the potential externalities of this policy toward reprocessing nuclear fuel for the purposes of national security. The capacity to reprocess fuel is prioritized over the potential health and environmental risks of an earthquake generated catastrophe at that plant.

The Fukushima disaster, in its entirety, but particularly in relation to the unit 3 reactor, demonstrates retroactively how the externalities of national security policies are privatized. Reactor 3, which was reported to be loaded with plutonium-enhanced MOX fuel at the time of the earthquake, was catastrophically damaged. The extent of plutonium

DOI: 10.1057/9781137343123

contamination is not fully known at this time, although plutonium from the Daiichi plant has been detected as far as Lithuania based on radioisotope analysis. Cesium from the plant has been detected widely in the United States, according to the U.S. Geological Survey.[72] Daiichi continues to emit radiation and conditions continue to deteriorate.[73] Hiroaki Koide, a nuclear reactor specialist and professor at Kyoto University, declared in July 2012 that "the state of the reactors is still deteriorating…the incident is still progressing."[74] Nuclear fallout from the Fukushima disaster demonstrates how risks from pursuing national security through nuclear will be borne primarily by civilian populations exposed to bio-accumulation of radioisotopes across time.

Notes

1   J. V. D. (1950) "Peaceful Uses of Atomic Energy," *The World Today*, 6.12, 521.
2   See H. J. Morgenthau (1960) "The Four Paradoxes of Nuclear Strategy," *The American Political Science Review*, 58.1, 23–35.
3   D. Elliott (2013*) Fukushima: Impacts and Implications* (Palgrave Pivot: Houndmills, Basingstoke), p. 66.
4   P. Bracken (2000) "The Second Nuclear Age," *Foreign Affairs*, 79.1, 146–150.
5   "Atomic Power Leads" (22 December 1945) *The Science News-Letter*, 48.25, 389–396.
6   D. Eisenhower "Atoms for Peace." Address to the 470th Plenary Meeting of the United Nations General Assembly, Tuesday, 8 December 1953, *The International Atomic Energy Agency (IAEA)*, http://www.iaea.org/About/history_speech.html, date accessed 7 June 2011.
7   W. Lanouette (1985) "Atomic Energy: 1945–1985," *The Wilson Quarterly*, 9.5, 100.
8   IAEA "IAEA Turns 40," p. 7.
9   Ibid.
10 Enrichment processing increases the proportion of uranium-235, which is fissile, to Uranium 238. A. Makhijani and S. Saleska (1999) *The Nuclear Power Deception* (The Apex Press: New York), p. 219.
11 Von Hippel "The Rise and Fall of the Plutonium Breeder Reactors," in T. Cochran, H. Feiveson, W. Patterson, G. Pshakin, M. Ramana, M. Schneider, T. Suzuki, and F. von Hippel (eds) *Fast Breeder Reactor Programs: History and Status: A Research Report of the International Panel on Fissile Materials* (pp. 1–16), http://fissilematerials.org/library/rro8.pdf, date accessed 17 2012, date accessed 17 July 2012.
12 Von Hippel "The Rise and Fall," p. 2.

DOI: 10.1057/9781137343123

13   Argonne National Laboratory (August 2005) "Plutonium," *Human Health Fact Sheet*, http://www.evs.anl.gov/pub/doc/Plutonium.pdf, date accessed 7 May 2012.

14   H. Caldicott (2006) *Nuclear Power Is Not the Answer* (The New Press: New York), 124.

15   von Hippel "The Rise and Fall of the Plutonium Breeder Reactors," p. 8.

16   S. Valentine and B. Sovacool (2010) "The Socio-Political Economy of Nuclear Power Development in Japan and South Korea," *Energy Politics*, 38, 7971–7979, p. 7973.

17   "Nuclear Law's 'National Security' Clause Must be Dropped" (22 June 2012) *The Asahi Shimbun*, http://ajw.asahi.com/article/views/editorial/AJ201206220037, date accessed 22 June 2012.

18   S. A. Khan (12 July 2012) "Japan's (Un)Clear Nuclear Ambition- Analysis," *Infectious Diseases Society of America*, http://www.eurasiareview.com/1207012-japans-unclear-nulcear-ambition-analysis/, date accessed 19 July 2012.

19   E. Warnock (1 June 2012) "Japan's Nuclear Industry: The CIA Link," *The Wall Street Journal*, http://blogs.wsj.com/japanrealtime/2012/06/01/japans-nuclear-industry-the-cia-link/, date accessed 1 June 2012.

20   "Japan's Citizen Kane: A Media Mogul Whose Extraordinary Life Still Shapes His Country, for Good and Ill" (22 December 2012), http://www.economist.com/news/christmas/21568589-media-mogul-whose-extraordinary-life-still-shapes-his-country-good-and-ill-japans, date accessed 22 December 2012.

21   P. Pringle and J. Spigelman (1981) *The Nuclear Barons*, 2nd edn (New York: Avon), p. 173.

22   Ibid., p. 174.

23   See H. Funabashi (2012) "Why the Fukushima Nuclear Disaster Is a Man-Made Calamity," *The International Journal of Japanese Sociology*, 21, 65–75. Also see Valentine and Sovacool "The Socio-Political Economy," p. 7974.

24   J. Trento (9 April 2012) "United States Circumvented Laws to Help Japan Accumulate Tons of Plutonium," *National Security News Service*, http://www.dcbureau.org/201204097128/national-security-news-service/united-states-circumvented-laws-to-help-japan-accumulate-tons-of-plutonium.html, date accessed 9 June 2012.

25   T. Suzuki (February 2010) "Japan's Plutonium Breeder Reactor and Its Fuel Cycle" in T. Cochran, H. Feiveson, W. Patterson, G. Pshakin, M. Ramana, M. Schneider, T. Suzuki, and F. von Hippel (eds) *Fast Breeder Reactor Programs: History and Status: A Research Report of the International Panel on Fissile Materials* (pp. 53–61), http://fissilematerials.org/library/rr08.pdf, date accessed 17 July 2012

26   W. Sweet (1988) "Japan's Nuclear Program Stresses Breeders, Plutonium, and Safeguards," *Physics Today*, 41.1, 71–74.

27   J. Daly (27 February 2012) "Another Fukushima Causality: Japan's Fast-Breeder Reactor Program," *Oil Price.Com*, http://oilprice.com/

DOI: 10.1057/9781137343123

alternative-energy/nuclear-power/another-fukushima-casualty-japans-fast-breeder-reactor-program.html, date accessed 8 June 2012.

28 Suzuki, "Japan's Plutonium Breeder Reactor and Its Fuel Cycle," p. 54.

29 "Monju Costs Far Surpass Usual Nukes: Trouble-Prone Reactor Has Rung up Far Higher Tab Than Initially Planned" (4 July 2012) *Japan Times*, http://www.japantimes.co.jp/text/nn20120704f1.html, date accessed 5 July 2012.

30 Daly, "Another Fukushima Causality."

31 S. Tatsujiro (2010) "Japan's Plutonium Breeder Reactor and Its Fuel Cycle," in T. B. Cochran, H. A. Feiveson., W. Patterson, G. Pshakin, M. V. Ramana, M. Schneider, T. Suzuki, F. von Hippel (eds) *Fast Breeder Reactor Programs: History and Status: A Research Report of the International Panel on Fissile Materials* (pp. 53–61), http://fissilematerials.org/library/rr08.pdf, date accessed 17 July 2012

32 Tatsujiro "Japan's Plutonium Breeder Reactor."

33 Trento "US Circumvented Laws to Help Japan Accumulate Tons of Plutonium."

34 Pringle and Spigelman, p. 325.

35 N. Shirouzu and C. Dawson (1 July 2011) "Design Flaw Fueled Nuclear Disaster," *The Wall Street Journal*, A1, A12.

36 Shirouzu and Dawson, "Design Flaw."

37 Shirouzu and Dawson, "Design Flaw," p. A12.

38 However, a status report issued by the IAEA on 5 May 2011, by Deputy Director General and Head of Department of Nuclear Safety and Security, Denis Flory, reported that as of 21 April, the exclusion zone around Fukushima Daini plant was reduced from 10 to kilometers. It is unclear why an exclusion zone around Daini was maintained through April if all the reactors there had shutdown safely.

39 "Fukushima: Mark 1 Nuclear Reactor Design Caused GE Scientist to Quit in Protest" (15 March 2011) ABC the Blotter, http://abcnews.go.com/Blotter/fukushima-mark-nuclear-reactor-design-caused-ge-scientist/story?id=13141287, date accessed 7 April 2011.

40 N. Shirouzu and A. Tudor (15 March 2011) "Crisis Revives Doubts on Regulation," *The Wall Street Journal*, http://online.wsj.com/article/SB10001424052748703363904576200533746195522.html, date accessed 15 March 2011.

41 Suzuki, "Japan's Plutonium Breeder Reactor and Its Fuel Cycle," p. 56.

42 "Heavy Fallout from Japan Nuclear Scandal" (2 September 2002), *CNN*, http://archives.cnn.com/2002/BUSINESS/asia/09/02/japan.TEPCO/index.html, date accessed 9 June 2012.

43 "Japan's Nuclear Power Operator Has Checkered Past" (12 March 2011), *Reuters*, http://www.reuters.com/article/2011/03/12/us-japan-nuclear-operator-idUSTRE72B1B420110312, date accessed 19 April 2011.

DOI: 10.1057/9781137343123

44   N. Shirouzu and R. Smith (16 March 2011) "Plant's Design, Safety Record Are under Scrutiny," *The Wall Street Journal*, http://online.wsj.com/article/SB10001 424052748704396504576204461929992144.html, date accessed 16 March 2011.

45   Shirouzu and Tudor, "Crisis Revives Doubts on Regulation."

46   "New Japanese Nuclear Power Reactors Delayed" (26 March 2008), *World Nuclear News*, http://www.world-nuclear-news.org/NN-New_Japanese_ nuclear_power_reactors_delayed-260308.html, date accessed 15 July 2012.

47   Shirouzu and Tudor "Crisis Revives Doubts on Regulation."

48   See S. Carpenter (2012) *Japan's Nuclear Crisis: The Routes to Responsibility* (Basingstoke and New York: Palgrave Macmillan), pp. 1–223.

49   "Hitachi Says Nuclear Power Sales to Double" (15 June 2012), *Japan Today*, http://www.japantoday.com/category/business/view/hitachi-says-nuclear-power-sales-to-double, date accessed 15 June 2012.

50   "Optimism Rises in 'Nuclear Village' after LDP's Victory" (19 December 2012), *The Asahi Shimbun*, http://ajw.asahi.com/article/0311disaster/ fukushima/AJ201212190048, date accessed 19 December 2012.

51   F. von Hippel and M. Takubo (28 November 2012) "Japan's Nuclear Mistake," *The New York Times*, http://www.nytimes.com/2012/11/29/opinion/japans-nuclear-mistake.html?nl=todaysheadlines&emc=edit_th_20121129&_r=0, date accessed 28 November 2012.

52   J. Takagi and B. Nishio (1990) "Nishio Japan's Fake Plutonium Shortage," *The Bulletin of Atomic Scientists*, 46.8, 34–38.

53   "Nuclear Law's 'National Security' Clause Must Be Dropped."

54   C. Dawson (8–9 December 2012) "Tokyo Shows off its Missile Defenses," *The Wall Street Journal*, A11.

55   C. Dawson (28 December 2011) "Japan Lifts Decades Long Ban on Export of Weapons," *The Wall Street Journal*, A8.

56   Dawson "Japan Lifts Decades Long Ban on Export of Weapons."

57   "PM Says Nuclear Deterrence Necessary for Japan" (6 August 2012), *BBC Monitoring Asia Pacific – Political*, http://www.lexisnexis.com.ezproxy1.lib.asu. edu/hottopics/lnacademic/, date accessed 7 November 2012.

58   "Atomic Energy Panel Members Call for Independent Probe into Secret Meetings" (29 May 2012), *The Mainichi*, http://mainichi.jp/english/english/ newsselect/news/20120529p2a00m0na010000c.html, date accessed 29 May 2012.

59   "The Black Box of Japan's Nuclear Power" (3 June 2012), *The Asia Pacific Journal*, http://www.japanfocus.org/events/view/151, date accessed 9 July 2012

60   "Nuclear Law's 'National security' Clause Must be Dropped.".

61   "Atomic Energy Law's Sly Alteration Is Abuse of Legislative Process" (26 June 2012), *The Mainichi*, http://mainichi.jp/english/english/perspectives/ news/20120626p2a00m0na004000c.html, date accessed 26 June 2012.

62   "Atomic Energy Law's Sly."

DOI: 10.1057/9781137343123

63   "National Security Clause Must be Deleted from Law on Atomic Energy" (23 June 2012), *The Mainichi*, http://mainichi.jp/english/english/perspectives/news/20120623p2a00m0na009000c.html, date accessed 25 June 2012.

64   Japan Sees Nuclear Power Plants as Powerful "Deterrent" against Foreign Attacks" (6 September 2012), *Newstrack India*, http://newstrackindia.com/newsdetails/2012/09/06/231-Japan-sees-nuclear-power-plants-as-powerful-deterrent-against-foreign-attacks.html, date accessed 9 February 2013.

65   Nuclear Control Institute (August 1990) "Reactor-Grade Plutonium's Explosive Properties," http://www.nci.org/NEW/NT/rgpu-mark-90.pdf, date accessed 6 February 2013.

66   P. Williamson (31 May 2012) "Plutonium and Japan's Nuclear Waste Problem: International Scientists Call for an End to Plutonium Reprocessing and Closing the Rokkasho Plant," *The Asia Pacific Journal*, http://japanfocus.org/-Piers-_Williamson/3766, date accessed 5 June 2012.

67   Von Hippel and Takubo "Japan's Nuclear Mistake."

68   "Industry Minister to Continue Nuclear Fuel Cycle Policy" (18 January 2013), *The Asahi Shimbun*, http://ajw.asahi.com/article/0311disaster/fukushima/AJ201301180037, date accessed 19 January 2013.

69   K. Hasegawa (19 December 2012) "Quake Risk at Japan Atomic Recycling Plant," *Pys.Org*, http://phys.org/news/2012–12-quake-japan-atomic-recycling-experts.html#jCp, date accessed 25 December 2012.

70   "72% of Newly Elected Lawmakers Want to Revise War-Renouncing Article 9 of Constitution" (18 December 2012), *The Mainichi,* http://mainichi.jp/english/english/newsselect/news/20121218p2a00m0na011000c.html, date accessed 18 December 2012.

71   Y. Hayashi, J. Page, and J. Barnes (6 February 2013) "Tensions Flare as Japan Says China Threatened Its Forces," *The Wall Street Journal*, A1, A9.

72   USGS (2012) *Fission Products in National Atmospheric Deposition Program-Wet Deposition Samples Prior to and Following the Fukushima Daiichi Nuclear Power Plant Incident, March 8–April 5, 2011.* Open File Report 2011–1277.

73   See T. Sugimoto (24 July 2012) "After 500 Days, Fukushima No. 1 Plant Still Not out of Woods," *The Asahi Shimbun*, http://ajw.asahi.com/article/0311disaster/fukushima/AJ201207240087, date accessed 24 July 2012.

74   Cited in K. Drubek (26 July 2012) "In Japan, a Nuclear Ghost Town Stirs to Life," *Open Channel NBC News.Com,* http://openchannel.nbcnews.com/_news/2012/07/26/12839675-in-japan-a-nuclear-ghost-town-stirs-to-life?lite, date accessed 7 August 2012.

DOI: 10.1057/9781137343123

3
Fukushima Disaster

Abstract: *The Fukushima nuclear disaster crisis management and policy responses are examined in relation to criticism raised by the Japanese Diet that TEPCO and the government failed to adequately protect citizens. The chapter's analysis of data on contamination in Japan and scientific findings of early effects on fauna suggest possibilities for significant intergenerational impacts. Yet, the risks of the disaster are essentially being privatized in myriad ways as citizens are required to assume the crisis externalities.*

Keywords: Fukushima nuclear disaster timeline, fallout and contamination in Japan, fallout effects on Japanese fauna, nuclear liability, and the privatization of risk

Holmer Nadesan, Majia. *Fukushima and the Privatization of Risk*. Basingstoke: Palgrave Macmillan, 2013.
DOI: 10.1057/9781137343123.

DOI: 10.1057/9781137343123

At the time of March 2011 earthquake, with a magnitude of 9 on the Richter scale, Japan had 54 operational nuclear power plants. The Fukushima nuclear site operated by TEPCO was reportedly hit hardest by the disastrous earthquake, and resultant tsunami. The site is approximately 160 miles north of Tokyo, located on the northeast coast. The complex comprises Fukushima Daiichi and Fukushima Daini, which are approximately six miles apart. Fukushima Daini has four nuclear reactors and Fukushima Daiichi has six reactors.

Each reactor has a spent fuel pool, in addition to a larger common spent fuel pool at Daiichi. These pools contain radioactive spent fuel rods. According to a 16 November report by TEPCO titled, "Integrity Inspection of Dry Storage Casks and Spent Fuel at Fukushima Daiichi Nuclear Power Station,"[1] as of March 2010 the Daini site held 1,060 tons of spent uranium fuel. The total spent uranium fuel inventory at Daiichi in March 2010 was reported as 1,760 tons. The 2010 report asserts that approximately 700 spent fuel assemblies are generated every year.[2] The report specifies that Daiichi's 3,450 assemblies are stored in each of the six reactor's spent fuel pools. The common spent fuel pool contains 6,291 assemblies. The amount of MOX fuel stored at the plant has not been reported.

In June 2011, Japan submitted a report to the IAEA indicating that fuel rods in reactors 1 through 3 had melted, breached inner containment vessels, and had accumulated in the outer containment vessels.[3] Doubt prevailed whether the other concrete containment could indefinitely stop melted corium.[4] TEPCO delayed reporting that full meltdowns had occurred in these reactors until three months after these events had transpired.[5] This type of underestimation was characteristic of much early crisis communications issued by TEPCO and government officials in Japan, the United States, and Canada.

One of the greatest risks identified early on in the disaster was the MOX fuel in reactor 3. Technical and media reports of the disaster indicate reactor 3's core contained a range of 32 to 164 MOX assemblies.[6] As the Fukushima 3/11 Watchdog group points out, the low-end estimate of 32 MOX assemblies translates into 5.5 tons of fuel containing more than 300 kg of plutonium.[7] Speaking at a press conference on 25 March 2011, Dr. Yablokov, lead contributor to *Chernobyl: Consequences of the Catastrophe for People and the Environment*, warned of the potential scale of the Fukushima disaster given plutonium fuel was involved:[8]

DOI: 10.1057/9781137343123

We are seeing something that has never happened – a multiple reactor catastrophe including one using plutonium fuel as well as spent fuel pool accidents, all happening within 200 kilometers of a metropolis of 30 million people. Because the area is far more densely populated than around Chernobyl, the human toll could eventually be far worse in Japan...I am not optimistic about the situation at Fukushima...It's especially dangerous if plutonium is released as inhalation of plutonium results in a high probability of cancer. A release of plutonium will contaminate that area forever and it is impossible to cleanup.

Also speaking at the press conference was Cindy Folkers, radiation and health specialist at Beyond Nuclear:

At Fukushima, our concern is not just the immediate exposures, but exposures that occur over the long term, from radioactive particles that are inhaled or ingested...These particles can fall on soil and in water and end up in the food supply for many years. We are worried that officials are measuring only the radiation that is the easiest to detect – gamma rays. Testing people for radiation on their skin or clothing is necessary, but it tells us little or nothing about what they could have breathed in or eaten – which results in internal exposure and long-term risk.

Dr. Yablokov concluded "When you hear 'no immediate danger' then you should run away as far and as fast as you can." Discussion begins with the timeline of events.

Timeline

Reactors 1 through 3 were operational at Fukushima Daiichi at the time of the earthquake.[9] The earthquake disrupted offsite power to the entire complex, triggering the emergency diesel generators. These diesel generators and switchgear rooms were subsequently flooded by a series of tsunamis, with heights reaching 49 feet.[10] All primary power was lost on units 1–4 and back-up power was lost on reactor units 1 and 2. Fukushima reactor number 1 exploded on Saturday, 12 March after venting failed to release pressure. The British newspaper *The Independent* reported that workers had seen cooling-water pipes burst after the earthquake and prior to the tsunami at 2:52 p.m. 11 March, indicating reactor damage and radiation releases prior to the tsunami.[11] It was eventually reported in *The Asahi Shimbun* that radiation levels on 12 March prior to the explosion of unit 1 had reached 1,590 microsieverts an hour in

DOI: 10.1057/9781137343123

Kamihatori in Futaba-machi, located 5.6 kilometers northwest of the Fukushima Daiichi plant.[12]

On Monday 14 March, a massive explosion occurred at the number 3 reactor.[13] After the explosion of reactor 3 was reported on 15 March, officials at the Fukushima plant assured that "there was no serious radiation leak, but acknowledged they had moved workers for safety reasons as a precaution."[14] Furthermore, officials noted that the "containment structures of the three reactors – which house the all-important reactor vessels – remained intact, preventing large-scale radiation leaks."[15] Later in the day on 15 March, an explosion occurred in reactor number 2. No definitive information about the state of the number 2 reactor was provided, although early news media reports described concerns about the integrity of the containment.[16] Reactor 4, which was not operating at the time of the disaster, was also damaged extensively, and fires were reported on 14 and 15 March, but specific details have never been released.

Decoding the full sequence of the events that occurred during the weeks after 11 March 2011 is an impossible task given the volume of conflicting reports about the extent and causes of damage at both the Fukushima Daiichi and Daini plants. The earliest reports indicated that five reactors were damaged across the two sites.[17] Yet, Japanese government spokesman Yukio Edano repeatedly assured that "There has been no meltdown" in order to prevent panic.[18]

Details in the press were confusing. For example, early press releases from TEPCO indicated that Daiichi unit 1 had only "mildly radioactive releases."[19] Later, it was reported it suffered a 70 percent fuel meltdown and was experiencing localized nuclear criticalities.[20] Ambiguity persisted regarding other reactor conditions. At the end of March, Japanese officials had reported they suspected only a "partial meltdown" had occurred in reactor 2,[21] despite earlier March reports of concerns about loss of containment there.[22] Later in 2012, TEPCO reported that unit 2 had been the primary source of radiation releases.[23] The status of Daiichi reactor 3 was particularly beset with confusion. Visual evidence indicates it had the largest explosion, but little information can be found about its actual status.

Smoke, not simply steam, was seen emanating from the building housing reactor 3 on 14 March. On 15 March, *The Los Angeles Times* reported: "Plumes of white smoke hung over the Fukushima nuclear complex Wednesday morning, possibly from the plant's No. 3 reactor. Officials for TEPCO said they did not know the cause of the smoke, but suggested it

DOI: 10.1057/9781137343123

could be steam."[24] Other photos released later of unit 3 revealed *blackish* smoke over that reactor building. *Dissensus Japan*, a Japanese site translating local stories into English, posted a comment made by Minamisoma City Council member Koichi Oyama about a mass of black smoke that stemmed from the reactor 3 explosion.[25] Reportedly, fallout from the black smoke continued for hours.

All of the spent fuel pools at the Fukushima Daiichi and Daini plants were imperiled by the loss of offsite power and the subsequent loss of generator power.[26] Spent fuel pools have been long acknowledged to pose significant dangers in nuclear emergencies because they contain tons and tons of highly reactive spent fuel rods that give off heat and therefore must be cooled constantly. A 2003 study of the hazards of spent fuel pools notes:

> Spent fuel recently discharged from a reactor could heat up relatively rapidly to temperatures at which the zircaloy fuel cladding could catch fire and the fuel's volatile fission products, including 30-year half-life 137Cs, would be released. The fire could well spread to older spent fuel. The long-term land-contamination consequences of such an event could be significantly worse than those from Chernobyl.[27]

These dangers were also documented in a 2005 report by the National Academy of Sciences. The radioactive contamination from fuel pools is so threatening because of the volume of fuel and the lack of containment. Given these known dangers, concerns were expressed early in the crisis that a fire in the spent fuel pools would release even more radiation than melted fuel in the actual reactors.[28] On 14 March, David A. Lochbaum, a nuclear engineer at the Union of Concerned Scientists, warned that the spent fuel of reactors 1 and 3 were "out in the open."[29]

Visual evidence of wreckage at unit 3 raised questions about whether its spent fuel pool was the source of the visible smoke given the degree of damage at that building.[30] Some early reports did state that TEPCO attributed the smoke to the spent fuel pool.[31] In a 17 March 2011 article in *The Wall Street Journal*, NRC Chairman Gregory Jaczko explained that he believed there was a crack in spent fuel pool 3. Nuclear engineer Arnie Gundersen subsequently reported in one of his video updates of the disaster that he believed the explosion at the number 3 reactor in March was caused by "prompt criticality" in number 3's fuel pool, rather than in the reactor itself.[32]

The conditions of other spent fuel pools at the Daiichi plant were never clarified. On 16 March it was reported that TEPCO officials were

DOI: 10.1057/9781137343123

warning that temperatures at the pools at reactors 5 and 6 were rising.[33] No follow up has been provided about these pools. Moreover, the status of the common spent fuel pool, which contained the most fuel by far, remains unclear. On 17 March 2011, *The Wall Street Journal* asserted that the status of common spent fuel pool holding 65 percent of used fuel rods from the Daiichi site was unknown.[34] The cooling system for the spent fuel pools at Fukushima Daini was also damaged, but no specific information was provided. The evacuation order for the area surrounding the Daini plant was based in part on concerns about these spent fuel pools overheating.[35]

The status of the spent fuel pool at reactor 4 was particularly clouded. On the morning of Tuesday 15 March, the IAEA released a statement warning that the Japanese authorities had reported a fire in spent fuel pool 4. Japanese authorities informed the IAEA at 03:50, coordinated universal time (UTC), that the spent fuel storage pond at the unit 4 reactor of the Fukushima Daiichi nuclear power plant was on fire and that radioactivity was being released directly into the atmosphere.[36] The fire was reportedly extinguished later on 15 March.[37] *The Los Angeles Times* reported this same sequence of fires in unit 4 spent fuel pool, which purportedly contained both new and spent fuel.[38] However, Jim Riccio, a nuclear expert for Greenpeace, reported on 16 March to *The Guardian* that the spent fuel pool at unit 4 was still boiling: "The spent fuel pool in unit 4 is boiling, and once that starts you can't stop it...The threat is that if you boil off the water, the metal cladding on the fuel rods that is exposed to the air, and is volatile, will catch fire. That will propel the radiation even further."[39] On 19 March, *The Los Angeles Times* reported that spent fuel pool 4 was still in danger of overheating because of cracks.[40] The chronology of events after this point becomes muddled as subsequent reports indicate that the pool was somehow repaired enough to contain water. On 20 June 2011, TEPCO reported that the water in spent fuel pool 4 was down by two-thirds as of 11 June and radiation levels were so high workers could not approach the pool.[41]

Over the next two years details about the status of spent fuel pool 4 at the time of the accident were slowly disclosed. In June 2012, the Chairman of Japan's Atomic Energy Agency admitted in an interview with *The Asahi Shimbun* that unit 4 had exploded, although specifics about the source and nature of the explosion were not provided.[42] On 8 March 2013, *The Japan Times* disclosed that unit 4's spent fuel pool contained MOX fuel at the time of the earthquake.[43] Still, the pool's status

DOI: 10.1057/9781137343123

remained unclear. Concerns about the potential for the pool to collapse entirely attracted international attention in the spring of 2012, as will be explained presently.

Release of the written transcripts of the 16 March audio files of the US Nuclear Regulatory Commission's Operation Center Fukushima Transcript provides some insight into the severities and complexities of the disaster. Conversations about the plant status clearly indicate that spent fuel pools 3 and 4 were damaged and burning.[44] On page 62 of the transcripts, speakers are recorded as stating that in addition to units 1 and 2 "boiling down," the spent fuel pools in 3 and 4 are having" zirc water reactions," indicating that the fuel cladding was burning because the used rods were no longer submerged in water. "No walls" on unit 4 spent fuel pool was noted: "The explosion leveled the walls, leveled the structure for the unit 4 spent fuel pool all the way down to the approximate level of the bottom of the fuel. So, there is no water in there whatsoever." Later in the transcripts, a speaker reiterated, "our understanding of the unit 4 spent fuel pool is it has been destroyed on the side such that it will get no water above the bottom of the active fuel for in effect the sides of the reactor building are gone...the sides are gone." The overall status of the plant is summarized on page 215 by another speaker: "2 reactors [in meltdown], multiple spent fuel pools and maybe 4 reactors and 4 spent fuel pools." The prognosis was considered grim: "We've just not seen any mitigation of any of the events and we would take all the spent fuel pools and probably all the four reactors into the final conclusion because we've not seen any mitigation."[45]

The site contamination complicated the emergency response. On 7 April 2011, *The New York Times* reported that broken fuel rods were found outside of containment at the Daiichi site: "Broken pieces of fuel rods have been found outside of Reactor No. 2, and are now being covered with bulldozers...The pieces may be from rods in the spent-fuel pools that were flung out by hydrogen explosions."[46] Fragments of rods were found up to one mile from the plant.[47] These highly radioactive rods are capable of producing immediately lethal doses of radiation.[48] It's not clear which reactor, reactors, or pools they came from. It *is* clear that plutonium was dispersed widely: In June 2011, *The Japan Times* reported a finding by Kanazawa University that plutonium from Fukushima was found in the town of Okuma about 1.7 km away from the plant's front gate.[49] Subsequently it was reported that plutonium from Fukushima was detected in ten locations in Fukushima Prefecture.[50]

DOI: 10.1057/9781137343123

As noted in Chapter 1, TEPCO claimed that the Daiichi plant was in "cold shutdown" in December 2011. However, detections of short-lived radioisotopes, such as Iodine-131, in November 2011 raised concerns that ongoing nuclear fission activity continued in damaged fuel at the plant, presenting grave dangers for workers.[51] In March 2011, physicist F. Dalnoki-Veress of the James Martin Center for Nonproliferation Studies at the Monterey Institute of International Studies posted his analysis of the possibility of ongoing and uncontrolled fission activity at the plant.[52] Dalnoki-Veress concluded from data on 13 neutron beam detections at Daiichi that pockets of melted fuel were producing transient criticalities, or nuclear fission events, significant enough to create the observed beams. He argued that the transient criticalities producing the beams are distinct from normal radioactive decay. He warned that TEPCO should be "aware of the possibility of transient criticalities when work is being done."

Although containment and cleanup efforts remain vague, some transparency was provided by the installation of video webcams trained on the Fukushima plant. The TEPCO webcam is located at the site and provides viewers a clear view of reactors 1 and 2 and a partial view of reactor 3. A second webcam, the TBS-JNN, is located on a hillside approximately ten miles from the plant. It offers viewers a clear view of the eastern side of the plant, revealing all four reactors. These webcams have allowed viewers ongoing access to the webcam videos, although censorship has been suspected by webcam watchers. Even so, these video feeds have disclosed probable fires that occurred at the plant in June 2011 and again in November 2011. Beginning in March 2012, large amounts of steam and smoke were viewed as coming from the general vicinities of the spent fuel pools for units 3 and 4.[53]

Fukushima Daiichi and Daini were not the only reactors reported damaged during the earthquake. A report titled "Lessons from Fukushima Dai-ichi" issued on 28 October 2011 by BBT University President Kenichi Ohmae, asserted that 14 nuclear reactors in Japan were extensively damaged by the earthquake.[54] Included in the list of damages is the nuclear "village" at Tokai where uranium enrichment occurs. Jim Walsh of MIT's Center of International Studies stated on 11 March 2011 that Japan's nuclear enrichment facilities in northern Japan were at risk, but that "no one has said 'boo' about them...It's not inconceivable that some of them have had problems."[55] *The New York Times* reported that fuel reprocessing at Rokkasho and a nuclear power plant at Higashidori in Aomori Prefecture

DOI: 10.1057/9781137343123

were running on emergency diesel generators after losing external power.[56] The Onagawa Nuclear Power Station in Miyagi Prefecture lost cooling temporarily at a spent fuel pool after losing two of its three external power systems. Additionally, Japanese blogger Ex-SKF reported on a fire at a depleted uranium storage facility that was in close proximity to a Cosmo Oil Refinery in Chiba that burned after the earthquake on 13 March 2011.[57] The facility owned by Chisso Petrochemical purportedly held 765 kilograms of depleted uranium at 0.3% concentration.

March atmospheric releases

As shall be elaborated upon further in this chapter, the volume of radiation released into the air and sea in March 2011 and over subsequent months has never been fully explicated. TEPCO stated and restated atmospheric emissions from March 2011 in reports ranging from a low of 440,000 terabecquerels to a reported high of 900,000 terabecquerels, which is "900 quadrillion Becquerels," or "17 zeros (a quadrillion is one thousand trillion)."[58] Figures have not been provided for the cumulative effect of over two years of ongoing steam and smoke emissions from the reactors. Japan's Metrological Research Institute scientists believe that 70 percent of radiation ended up in the sea. Even so, atmospheric levels over land were extraordinarily high. For instance, soil sample data collected at the Canadian Embassy in Tokyo on March 23 2011 was used to extrapolate total fallout inventory at this point in time at 225,000 Bq/m2.[59]

A study released in *Scientific Reports* published by *Nature* titled "Isotopic Evidence of Plutonium Release into the Environment from the Fukushima DNPP Accident" by Zheng et al. found that a wide array of highly volatile fission products were released, including ^{129m}Te, ^{131}I, ^{134}Cs, ^{136}Cs and ^{137}Cs, which were all found to be "widely distributed in Fukushima and its adjacent prefectures in eastern Japan."[60] The study also found evidence of actinides, particularly Pu isotopes, on the ground northwest and south of the Fukushima DNPP in the 20–30 km zones. The study called for long-term investigation of Pu and ^{241}Am dose estimates because of findings of "high activity ratio of ^{241}Pu/$^{239}+^{240}$Pu (> 100) from the Fukushima DNPP accident." The study concluded that in comparison to Chernobyl, the Fukushima accident "had a slightly higher ^{241}Pu/^{239}Pu atom ratio, but lower ratio of ^{240}Pu/^{239}Pu." Unit 3 was seen as the likely source for the high Pu detections.

DOI: 10.1057/9781137343123

It is believed that radioisotopes released by the plant were absorbed into aerosol particles with durable molecular structures, facilitating long-distance transport.[61] Contributing to this conclusion is research by Armstrong et al., which demonstrates that the use of salt water to cool the reactors likely produced spherical, uranium peroxide clusters.[62] These clusters, described as buckyballs, have high durability and transportability. Another study found evidence of Sulfur-35 (^{35}S) in sulfate aerosol thousands of miles away in southern California from 20 to 28 March 2011.[63] The researchers concluded that neutron leakage transformed salt water chlorine (^{35}Cl) into radioactive ^{35}S through a process of multistage decay. Fukushima contamination may have spread more widely across the northern hemisphere because of the composition and durability of the radioactive aerosols produced. A U.S. Geological Survey published in 2012 documents evidence of wet deposition of fission products in the western United States.[64]

Despite significant releases of radiation in the early days of the disaster, TEPCO and the Japanese government offered reassuring words to panicked citizens. As Professor Robert Jacobs, Hiroshima Peace Institute, Hiroshima City University declared, "They tried to keep the word meltdown off of the headlines" until the story had lost relevance in international news headlines.[65]

Crisis communications and evacuations in Japan

During the summer of 2012 Japan's National Diet issued "The Official Report of the Fukushima Nuclear Accident Independent Investigation Commission." On page 9 of the executive summary, the report describes the disaster primarily human wrought:

> THE EARTHQUAKE AND TSUNAMI of March 11, 2011 were natural disasters of a magnitude that shocked the entire world. Although triggered by these cataclysmic events, the subsequent accident at the Fukushima Daiichi Nuclear Power Plant cannot be regarded as a natural disaster. It was a profoundly manmade disaster – that could and should have been foreseen and prevented. And its effects could have been mitigated by a more effective human response...Our report catalogues a multitude of errors and willful negligence that left the Fukushima plant unprepared for the events of March 11. And it examines serious deficiencies in the response to the accident by TEPCO, regulators and the government.[66]

DOI: 10.1057/9781137343123

The willful negligence was examined previously in this chapter in relation to the fabrication of safety data by TEPCO officials. The "serious deficiencies in the response to the accident" will be briefly examined in this section.

Three main problems with the government and TEPCO response included lack of adequate safety preparations prior to the disaster; lack of adequate evacuations during the disaster; and evacuation of people into the plume. Inadequate disaster planning stemmed in part from concerns that antinuclear activists would use accident scenarios to mobilize resistance. In November 2012 *The Asahi Shimbun* reported: "TEPCO acknowledged for the first time last month, in a document outlining company reforms, that it had failed to anticipate and tackle the March 2011 disaster. It said it had feared that implementing accident measures would alarm the public and boost Japan's antinuclear movement."[67] The Japanese Diet report describes how poor planning confounded efforts to evacuate residents to safe areas:

> Evacuation issues: The Commission concludes that the residents' confusion over the evacuation stemmed from the regulators' negligence and failure over the years to implement adequate measures against a nuclear disaster, as well as a lack of action by previous governments and regulators focused on crisis management. The crisis management system that existed for the Kantei and the regulators should protect the health and safety of the public, but it failed in this function.[68]

These evacuation problems occurred because of the unwillingness of TEPCO and the Japanese government to acknowledge the scale of the disaster and to release information about plume data for fear of panicking residents. On 11 March at 20:50 the Japanese government ordered people within a two-kilometer radius of the plant to evacuate. Later in the day, this evacuation zone was extended to a three-kilometer radius of the Fukushima I plant.[69] On 12 March, the three-kilometer evacuation order was repeated, and then extended to ten kilometers later in the day, but the Diet report documents that residents were not provided information about where to go. The evacuation order was finally extended to a 20-kilometer radius at 18:25 UTC.[70] This evacuation zone was inadequate and information about where to evacuate resulted in the movement of people into the plume, rather than away from it. In fact, the Diet report charges that some people evacuated into higher radiation areas where they remained until April.[71] On 22 April, Japan's central government designated five municipalities in Fukushima Prefecture for evacuation.[72]

DOI: 10.1057/9781137343123

The limited evacuations were a result of official efforts to minimize public perceptions of the scope of the disaster. Japanese authorities and other officials insisted that there was little to no danger during the midst of the Fukushima disaster. On 12 March 2011, University of Tokyo Professor Naoto Sekimura appeared repeatedly on Japanese television to reassure local residents that all was under control. CNN repeated Sekimura's comments: "Only a small part of the fuel may have melted and leaked outside...most of the fuel remains inside the reactor, which has stopped operating and is being cooled."[73] On 13 March, after the first explosion, the World Health Organization reported that the risk from the reactors was "probably quite low."[74] Even as late as April 2011, when TEPCO knew that complete core meltdowns had occurred, a former nuclear regulator who had served as a consultant to TEPCO claimed publicly that there was no danger as total meltdowns had not occurred.[75]

Japanese citizens were left confused and worried, uncertain about how far to evacuate and where to go. Kazunobu Sakurai, the mayor of Minamisoma, told Japan's *NHK* on 15 March that "The government and Tokyo Electric Power have neglected to update residents with accurate information ...We need the government to keep us informed, to send emergency supplies and to help move residents who are inside the evacuation zone."[76] However, it was not until 25 March that the Japanese government declared a *voluntary* evacuation for people within 30 kilometers of the plant while the official evacuation zone remained 20 kilometers.[77] Exacerbating Japanese citizens' uncertainty about how far to evacuate was the U.S. recommendation made on 17 March that U.S. citizens and troops stay at least 50 miles from the Fukushima reactors.[78] On 4 April, *The Wall Street Journal* reported that Japanese authorities had finally acknowledged that the evacuation zone needed to be expanded beyond 30 kilometers.[79]

Some critics of the crisis management charge that deliberate censorship was employed by the Japanese government to reduce public concern about the disaster. Fujioka Atsushi, a professor of economics at Ritsumeikan University and Planning Director for the Kyoto Museum for World Peace, claimed *NHK* censored images in Japan of the explosion and black smoke in the shape of a mushroom cloud at Daiichi's unit 3 reactor.[80] Atsushi decried the censorship, comparing it with what had occurred during the final days of World War II: "A news blackout was imposed that resembled the days of the Pacific War, when only official bulletins could be reported."

DOI: 10.1057/9781137343123

Indeed, it took Japanese officials over a month to disclose large-scale radiation releases occurring at the Fukushima plant in mid-March.[81] Japan used a system called Speedi – System for Prediction of Environmental Emergency Dose information – to model March radiation releases and blamed the delay in reporting results to the public in mid-April on their efforts to narrow the margin of error in their calculations, although nuclear regulators in other countries were privy to Speedi's results early on.[82] In July 2011, the Atomic Energy Society of Japan, an academic group, publicly criticized the Japanese government and TEPCO for delays in reporting Speedi data to the public, as illustrated here:

> The society notes that there is the possibility that the damage to people's health from radiation exposure has increased because the government, TEPCO and other related institutions did not properly disclose information on the status of the nuclear accidents and the environmental contamination by radioactive substances. It says that although they had information that must be disclosed, they have not done so. An example that surfaced recently is the education and science ministry's failure to immediately disclose the name of a radiation hot spot in Namie, Fukushima Prefecture.[83]

As asserted here, the delay and underestimation of the radiation released by the plant resulted in an inadequate evacuation zone. *Japan Today* reported in August 2011 that Japan's radiation detection systems were working from the first moment of the disaster when the plant decided to vent radiation, but that the data were disregarded despite the fact that projections indicated that Karino Elementary School would be immediately in the path of the plume, leading to the irradiation of about 400 students, teachers, and parents.[84] Again, in 2012, the Japanese media criticized their government for failing to release Speedi fallout simulations.[85] Fears of panic and public disorder were prioritized over public safety risks posed by radiation exposure.

Confusion about the imminence of risk and the threat of panic led to delays and failures by officials to distribute potassium iodide pills, which can block thyroid absorption of radioiodine.[86] Local officials had the pills on-hand, but policy dictated they wait for the central government to give the official order. Records indicate that Tokyo didn't order distribution of the pills until five days after the disaster. Nearly 100,000 residents had already evacuated by that time. Children's exposure to radioiodine could have been mitigated had the pills been distributed in a timely manner.

In June 2012 *The Asahi Shimbun* revealed that some agencies within Japan also had detailed real-time readings of radiation dispersion

DOI: 10.1057/9781137343123

plumes for the period ranging from 17 March through 19 March provided by the U.S. government, but that the information was not made available to the prime minister.[87] The U.S. Energy Department had used its Aerial Measuring System to create detailed maps of radiation levels over affected areas in Japan, based on actual aerial detections, rather than computer modeling.[88] The U.S. data were sent to Japan's Foreign Ministry, who forwarded it to NISA and the science ministry. The article notes that the data were not shared with the prime minister's office, or the Nuclear Safety Commission (NSC). Dr. Tokushi Shibata, professor emeritus of radiation management at the University of Tokyo was quoted as stating: "It was a fatal error in judgment. If the data had been released immediately, the situation of residents evacuating in the wrong direction and becoming exposed to radiation could have been avoided." When *The Asahi Shimbun* asked why the information was not used to implement evacuation plans, Watanabe (the deputy director general of the Science and Technology Policy Bureau), said: "While I now feel that the information should have been released immediately, at that time there was no thought given to using the provided data for the benefit of evacuating residents. We should have also passed on the information to the NSC."[89]

Contamination

In 2011, former senior policy advisor to the U.S. Secretary of Energy, Robert Alvarez, argued that 600 square kilometers were "technically uninhabitable" because of Cesium-137 contamination.[90] A 26 June 2011 survey of soil in Fukushima City found all samples contaminated with cesium levels exceeding legal limit of 10,000 Becquerels per square meter.[91] Data from Japan dated September 2011 documented 2,000 square kilometers in Japan to have radiation contamination levels at or in excess of one microsievert per hour at a measured height of 0.5 to 1.0 meter,[92] leading to an annual external exposure rate of 8.76 millisieverts from soil contamination alone. Fujioka Atsushi explained that a map released jointly by Japanese Ministry of Education, Culture, Sports and Science (MEXT) and the U.S. Department of Energy measuring levels of soil radiation at 150 to 700 meters above the ground indicated accumulations of Cesium-137 exceeding 600,000 Becquerels per square meter for 800 square kilometers.[93] This level of contamination led to mandatory

DOI: 10.1057/9781137343123

evacuations during the Chernobyl accident. Atsushi argued the severity of the contamination was downplayed in order to reduce evacuations. *The Asahi Shimbun* corroborated his concerns, concluding in 2013: "The government avoided setting stringent radiation reference levels for the return of Fukushima evacuees for fear of triggering a population drain and being hit by ballooning costs for compensation."[94]

One ongoing concern about fallout is food contamination. Although farmers and local civic authorities may check for food contamination, Japan has no centralized system for checking radiation contamination.[95] Testing by local prefectural governments, farmers, and distributors have found contamination of tea, beef, rice, milk, and other items. For instance, radioactive cesium exceeding the Japanese government's upper limits were found in Japanese black cattle shipped from a farm in the Fukushima prefecture in July 2011.[96] Animals with radioactive emissions up to 100,000 counts per minute were considered safe by Japan's health authorities. At 100,000 counts per minute, a human would require full-body decontamination.[97] Tea, Japan's national beverage, has also been found to be contaminated by cesium.[98] Cesium bio-accumulates in plants because it is a potassium analog and it bio-magnifies as it moves up the food chain, across species.[99] Tap water, in addition to food, may become in Japan a pathway for exposure. On 23 August 2012, MEXT measured detectable levels of Cesium-134 and 137 in tap water of 12 of the 46 prefectures sampled between April and June of 2012.[100]

Contamination in Japan was exacerbated by the decision to burn radioactive waste, as described by *The Mainichi* in September 2011.[101] In November 2011, radioactive ash caused incinerators in Kashiwa (Chiba Prefecture) to shut down because of the challenges of storing the highly contaminated debris.[102] Levels of contamination reached 70,800 Becquerels of cesium per kilogram (Bk/kg), as measured by radiation checks conducted at two incineration plants and one disposal facility. *The Mainichi* reported in April 2012 that Fukushima would begin burning 453,592,333 kg of radioactive waste measuring 100,000 Bq/kg in the exclusion zone.[103] Residents in Fukushima City promptly protested these plans.[104] In November 2012, Japan announced plans to transport 13 million tons of debris 400 kilometers away from Fukushima to be ground up into mulch and burned, despite widespread citizen resistance across Japan.[105] It is not altogether clear why Japan has selected incineration given this practices does not eliminate or reduce radioactivity of waste and may spread radiation contamination in the atmosphere.[106] Indeed,

DOI: 10.1057/9781137343123

one study of incinerator ash from Fukushima contaminated debris estimated that 88 percent of the total radioactive cesium in the debris was at
risk for elution and diffusion with wind and rain.[107]

Inadequate evacuations and spotty testing of soil, food, and water
resulted in radiation contamination of Japanese citizens still living in
close proximity to the plant. A study measuring thyroid exposure to
Iodine-131 conducted between 12 April and 16 April 2011 published in
Research Reports found "extensive measurements of the exposure to I-131
revealing I-131 activity in the thyroid of 46 out of the 62 residents and
evacuees measured."[108] *NHK* reported in March 2012 that researchers
from Hirosaki University in Aomori Prefecture had detected in April
2011 radioactive iodine in the thyroid glands of 80 percent of the 65
people sampled who formerly lived in close proximity to the Fukushima
nuclear plant.[109]

By June 2011, radioactive contamination could be detected in the
urine of residents still living within the Fukushima prefecture[110] and
residents were still living in Fukushima City, despite soil contamination
readings far exceeding levels used by the Soviets to mandate compul-
sory resettlements after the 1986 Chernobyl disaster.[111] Concerns have
therefore been expressed that Japan has failed to adequately protect
citizens from internal contamination. In a *Democracy Now* interview on
3 June 2011, Aileen Mioko Smith, executive director of Green Action,
described comments made by Dr. Shunichi Yamashita, the appointed
radiological health safety risk management adviser for the Fukushima
prefecture:

> [Aileen Mioko Smith]: Yes, we're very concerned that a health study is start-
> ing at the end of this month. This is concerning the effects of the Fukushima
> residents, on the prefectural citizens. It's headed by a Dr. Shunichi
> Yamashita, who's at the Atomic Bomb Research Institute...He's widely
> shown on national TV. He speaks widely in the prefecture, always saying
> there's absolutely no concern with the levels of radiation in Fukushima.
> He says that mothers, even mothers exposed to 100 millisieverts, pregnant
> mothers, will not have any effect, health effect. Remember the number 100.
> Compared to that, the Soviet Union required a mandatory evacuation dur-
> ing Chernobyl at five millisieverts. This doctor is quoted as saying, "The
> effects of radiation do not come to people that are happy and laughing.
> They come to people that are weak-spirited, that brood and fret." This is a
> direct quote. And he's heading the study. And so, the citizens in Fukushima
> are very concerned.[112]

DOI: 10.1057/9781137343123

In a subsequent interview with *Der Spiegel*, Dr. Yamashita was pressed to explain his assertion that no effects from radiation occur when people are happy. He responded by claiming that there exists little statistically significant increased rates of cancer for exposure levels under 100 millisieverts.[113] This assertion will be examined in Chapter 4's discussion of the biological effects of radiation. For now, it's instructive to compare this level of 100 millisieverts represented as safe by Dr. Yamashita for pregnant women with the five millisieverts a year level of exposure used by the Soviets after Chernobyl to dictate evacuation of citizens.[114]

A year later, in June 2012, reports of highly radioactive black soil began appearing in Japan. On 14 June *The Asahi Shimbun* ran a story addressing the soil:

> The highest level of radioactivity detected – about 5.57 million becquerels per kilogram – came from black soil collected in the Kanaya neighborhood of the Odaka district of southern Minami-Soma. In 36 out of 41 locations in Fukushima Prefecture where black soil was collected, the radioactivity level exceeded 100,000 becquerels per kilogram. If that level was found in incinerator ash, it would have to be handled very carefully and buried in a facility that had a concrete exterior separating it from its surroundings.[115]

Citizens concerned about the highly radioactive soil brought samples to Tomoya Yamauchi, an academic specializing in radiation measurement. Yamauchi found that the soil contained radioactive cesium at levels of 1.08 million Bq/kg. Other samples of soil brought in from Minamisoma contained plutonium and strontium. Tokyo also yielded samples of highly radioactive soil. Despite the high levels of radiation, the article reported action was not being taken to remove the soil:

> But for now, nothing is being done about the black soil with high levels of radiation. "Because it normally is found on the ground, we believe it is not something that will have immediate effects on human health," a Minami-Soma municipal government official said.

No "immediate effects on human health" had become an often-chanted mantra.

A variety of citizens, NGOs, and international activists have conducted their own monitoring of radiation levels in order to evaluate safety assurances. One finding has been that radiation emissions from the plant are ongoing. Dr. Chris Busby reported on the Russian television network *RT* on 17 August 2011 that ongoing plant emissions at the time were reported to the Japanese prime minister by TEPCO to be continuing 10 to the 13th

DOI: 10.1057/9781137343123

power Becquerels per hour.[116] Likewise, during an interview with Dr. Helen Caldicott, broadcasted online in September 2011, Arnie Gundersen stated that he had been told that Fukushima was currently emitting a gigabecquerel per day (gigabecquerel or GBq 10^9 Bq), in radiation, which he described as over two billion decays per second a day.[117]

Official TEPCO and Japanese government measures of contamination have been called into question by independent researchers and citizens armed with radiation detectors. For example, the Japanese blogger Ex-SKF reported that a radiation survey reported in late July 2011 by Doshisha University and Kyoto Seika University of Fukushima City (in Fukushima Prefecture) found 56.9 microsieverts/hour at an elementary school and 20.8 microsieverts/hour at the Fukushima Prefectural Government building.[118] Japanese officials refused to expand evacuations despite significantly high radiation level detections by citizens 150 kilometers from the plant.[119]

In 2012, a group of Japanese citizens, The Association for Citizens and Scientists Concerned about Internal Radiation Exposure, argued that their own radiation readings at monitoring posts set up by MEXT were between 10 and 50 percent higher than the ministry's numbers.[120] Translating Japanese media reports, two Japanese bloggers, Ex-SKF and Fukushima Diary, reported in November 2012 that the Japanese government acknowledged that radiation readings in Fukushima were reduced by 10 percent in 675 monitoring posts because the detectors' batteries were shielding the sensors from radiation.[121] Finally, there have been ongoing allegations that official radiation levels were manipulated. Early in the disaster, former minister for Internal Affairs Haraguchi Kazuhiro alleged that radiation monitoring station data was actually three decimal places greater than the numbers released to the public.[122]

Over a year after the initial meltdown, Fukushima's reactors and spent fuel pools continue to emit radiation daily and TEPCO struggled to prevent re-criticalities and hydrogen explosions.[123] TEPCO has injected nitrogen into reactors 2 and 3 in order to prevent another hydrogen explosion on more than one occasion.[124] A media blackout persisted on the exact condition and status of spent fuel pools of reactor units 3 and 4, although large amounts of steam and possibly smoke could be seen released from their general vicinities on TEPCO's live video cam trained on the Fukushima plants.[125] Continuing to hold relevance is Japanese American physicist Dr. Kaku's description of Fukushima as a "ticking time bomb" capable of more massive releases.[126]

DOI: 10.1057/9781137343123

Japanese children

In April 2011, Japan's government increased the safe exposure level for children from one millisievert a year to 20 millisieverts a year, which is the level recommended by the International Commission on Radiological Protection (ICRP) for nuclear plant workers, far exceeding the recommended public health limit of one millisievert per year,[127] despite evidence that children are at the very least ten times more vulnerable to the deleterious effects of ionizing radiation.[128] This decision caused Japan's Professor Toshiso Kosako, who was temporarily appointed to the government's nuclear advisory committee, to resign in protest over the "intolerable" new level.[129] The Say-Peace Project, under the editorial supervision of Dr. Matsui Eisuke, Director of the Gifu Environmental Medicine Research Institute, charged that a pamphlet published on 2 April 2011 by the Ministry of Health, Labor, and Welfare "assured pregnant women and the mothers of small children that 'there is no need to worry,' without providing any scientific basis for the claim."[130] In response to this kind of public pressure, the Japanese government's education ministry subsequently reduced the allowable level of radiation from outdoor school activities to one millisievert during the summer of 2011.[131]

Still, Japanese children are exposed to fallout in their homes, schools, and parks. In the not evacuated areas of Fukushima Prefecture, parents and teachers voluntarily removed the topsoil from contaminated school yards even though officials declared the soil contamination levels "safe." Japanese school children approximately 60 kilometers from the stricken Fukushima plant were given radiation meters five full months after the crisis began.[132] Yet, (unconfirmed) reports had begun surfacing as early as June 2011 that children in heavily impacted areas were suffering radiation health effects. The Japanese blogger Ex-SKF translated a newspaper report from June 2011 addressing inexplicable illnesses in children living within 50 kilometers of the plant:

> Tokyo Shinbun [paper edition only, 6/16/2011] reports that many children in Koriyama City in Fukushima Prefecture, 50 kilometers from Fukushima I Nuclear Power Plant, are suffering inexplicable nosebleed, diarrhea, and lack of energy since the nuke plant accident.[133]

Anecdotal reports of nose bleeds, diarrhea, and fatigue continued to circulate over the next year and a half in tweets by individuals, nurses, and citizen groups.

DOI: 10.1057/9781137343123

Kodama Tatsuhiko, head of the Radioisotope Center at the University of Tokyo, emphasized the special risks posed by radiation to children when speaking before Japanese Diet members in July 2012, explaining that their rapid cell division makes them more vulnerable to DNA mutations.[134] He cautioned that radiation badges and whole body scans are inadequate for measuring risks because internally ingested radioisotopes such as Cesium-137 and Iodine-131 are not found uniformly across the body, but rather are concentrated in organs. He explained that it takes years for cancers to develop after exposure and that efforts to prove that exposure caused subsequent illnesses require data from control groups, allowing comparisons to be drawn from baseline normal incidences of disease rates within populations.

Evidence exists that children in Fukushima have been contaminated internally with radiocesium. The Fukushima Network for Saving Children from Radiation took samples from ten elementary through high-school children in the spring of 2011.[135] Analysis detected Cesium-134, of up to 1.13 Becquerels per liter in their urine. The organization stated that children living within 60 kilometers from the plant suffer from internal radiation exposure. When reporting on this news, *NHK* reassured readers that "The Japanese non-profit Radiation Effects Research Foundation says no health problems due to such radiation levels have been reported, and that people should not be overly concerned."[136] On 1 July 2012 *Kyodo News* reported that radioactive cesium was detected in the urine of 141 children out of 2,022 surveyed in Fukushima Prefecture.[137] Samples contained more than 10 Bq/kg of cesium. One sample registered at 17.5 Bq/kg. Detections of radioactive potassium were also documented, averaging at about 64 Bq/kg. Samples were analyzed by the Yokohama-based Isotope Research Institute.

In a 2003 video titled Nuclear Controversies by Vladimir Tchertkoff,[138] Professor Yury Bandazhevsky (former director of the Medical Institute in Gomel) states that based on his research on children exposed to radiocesium from Chernobyl, "Over 50 Bq/kg of body weight lead to irreversible lesions in vital organs." In a short summary of his work published in 2003, Bandazhevsky described high levels of Cesium-137 bio-accumulation in Chernobyl children's heart and endocrine glands, particularly the thyroid gland, the adrenals, and the pancreas.[139] He also found high levels in the thymus and the spleen. He concluded that higher levels of bio-accumulation were found in children than adults.

Children's exposure to radioiodine is also of particular concern because it bio-accumulates in organs. Kodama Tatsuhiko warned that research

DOI: 10.1057/9781137343123

from Chernobyl retroactively established that thyroid cancer resulted from radioiodine concentration in children's thyroid.[140] Thyroid cancer caused by exposure to radioiodine can be treated, but requires lifetime interventions. Considerable uncertainty exists over Japanese children's actual levels of exposure to Iodine-131, which has a short, eight-day half-life. As mentioned previously in this chapter, many Japanese children were not given potassium iodide pills in a timely fashion to prevent absorption of radioiodine. Research led by Toshikazu Suzuki of Japan's National Institute of Radiological Sciences (NIRS) looked at data that modeled the hourly thyroid dose of over a 1,000 children under 16 years of age in Fukushima Prefecture from March 24 to March 30. The study estimated the children's thyroid dose at between 12 and 42 millisieverts from Iodine-131 alone.[141] However, these results were later called into question for underestimating exposure levels because the study relied on estimates of radioiodine, rather than actual measurements.[142] In August 2011, *NHK* reported that Japan's nuclear commission had erased children's exposure data derived from a test of 1,000 children aged 15 or younger who had been screened for radiation affecting their thyroid.[143] It appears, although cannot be verified, that the erased data was from the NIRS study.

Perhaps the clearest evidence of children's exposure to radioiodine is subsequent detections of thyroid nodules. In April 2012, the Peace Philosophy Centre posted the results of the Fukushima government's March 2012 survey of 38,001 children under 18 located in 13 Fukushima Prefecture cities. Thyroid nodules (5.0mm) or cyst (20.0mm) were detected in 13,460 individuals, or 35.3 percent of the sample. These results were an increase of 5.6 percent from a January pre-test.[144] Confirmation of findings were found in the data reported by the Sixth Report of Fukushima Prefecture Health Management Survey, documenting that nearly 36 percent of Fukushima children had abnormal growths on their thyroids.[145] *The Guardian* reported in February 2013 that "Japan has tested 133,000 children in Fukushima and found abnormal thyroid cysts and nodules in 42% of them. Three cases of cancer were confirmed and another seven were suspected cases 'with an 80% chance of malignancy.'"[146]

Evidence of the Fukushima children's ongoing internal contamination is perhaps the greatest tragedy of this disaster. Activists had called for evacuations of children and pregnant women in the first months of the disaster because of their special susceptibilities.[147] Yet, as established here, evacuation orders were not timely and wide enough to prevent contamination. For this reason it was particularly concerning when

DOI: 10.1057/9781137343123

allegations began surfacing in the fall of 2012 of manipulation of government tests results of thyroid nodule detections in Fukushima children.

An independent blogger and filmmaker, Ian Thomas Ash, began documenting Fukushima families' experiences in November 2012 at his blog for his film *A2*, the title of which refers to a positive diagnosis for thyroid tumors.[148] In a 5 November post at his blog titled, "The Mothers and Their Children," Ash explained:

> This morning I met Mrs. Shima. She had invited several other mothers over to her home to share with me their situations and the thyroid test results for their children. Mrs. Shima showed me the thyroid ultrasound for her daughter Shuri, 11. The government-sponsored test revealed her daughter had NO thyroid cysts, but she went to a private hospital to seek a second opinion. She was told her daughter in fact DOES have thyroid cysts. In both tests, it was discovered that her son Kaito, 13, also has thyroid cysts.[149]

Although authentication of this report is difficult, other observers have reported similar findings. Steve Zeltzer, a videographer and journalist producer at KPFA Radio on the Pacifica Network, visited Fukushima in the fall of 2012 and found mothers who had been pressured by doctors to disregard troubling health symptoms in their children.[150] He found residents being pressured to return to their homes, even those who formerly lived as close as four miles from Daiichi.

Radioiodine doesn't simply affect the thyroid, where it bio-accumulates. It is also known to have especially detrimental gestation effects. Research published by Dr. Alfred Koerblein in 2013 reported a significant three-fold increase of infant mortality in Fukushima Prefecture in May 2011 ($O = 9$, $E = 3.1$, $P = 0.0014$).[151] Pronounced peaks in infant mortality were also found in Fukushima for December 2011. Koerblein noted *significant reductions in the number of live births in December 2011 in Japan as a whole.* He concluded that the falling birth rate could be caused by radiation-induced loss of zygotes shortly after fertilization. This study and Koerblein's previous research on Chernobyl demonstrate the radiation susceptibility of developing beings, with the youngest being most vulnerable.[152]

On 24 April 2013, the Japanese Sendai High Court rejected an international lawsuit demanding evacuation of Fukushima children.[153] The lawsuit, filed by Fukushima Prefecture children, their parents, and antinuclear activists, demanded that children be evacuated from the city of Koriyama to an area of Japan with "no higher than natural background levels" of radiation.[154] The court did acknowledge that radiation levels were higher than those deemed unsafe prior to the disaster. However, it rejected the

DOI: 10.1057/9781137343123

evacuation demand by asserting limits on the government's evacuation responsibilities. It is believed likely that the decision will be appealed.

Plant workers at Daiichi

Work at the Fukushima Daiichi plant has been very dangerous. TEPCO has relied on paid workers and volunteers; however, many workers at the plant have claimed they were not told where they would be working when hired. During the early days of the disaster workers did not receive dosimeters to monitor their radiation exposure.[155] The command center used by workers during cleanup was subsequently revealed to be contaminated, potentially causing thousands of workers to ingest radioactive particles. One worker waded into radioactive water and was burned because he was not wearing appropriate protection. Workers were not required to wear waterproof ponchos when it rained, although rainwater is known to wash out radioactive contamination in the air.

Testing of workers found hundreds were contaminated. In December 2012, *The Asahi Shimbun* reported that TEPCO found 178 workers whose thyroid glands evidenced exposure levels exceeding 100 millisieverts.[156] One hundred and sixty-three workers were calculated to have had thyroid doses exceeding 200 millisieverts. The highest dose recorded was 11,800 millisieverts, although two workers were found with exposure levels over 10,000 millisieverts.

Ilya Perlingieri described these workers as expendable in her essay "No Protection for Fukushima's Expendable Citizens or Us":

> On March 14, the Japanese industry of Health and Labor raised "the maximum [radiation] dose for workers to 250 mSv [millisieverts] a year" an increase in exposure from the previous 100 mSv. These new figures are also drastically higher than those from the International Commission on Radiological Protection's guidelines stipulating a maximum of 20 mSv a year.[157]

The Mainichi reported on 22 June 2011 that the whereabouts of 30 former Fukushima plant workers were unknown: "The workers' names were listed in records showing that they had been loaned dosimeters, but when the plant's operator, TEPCO, contacted the companies they were associated with, the companies replied that there was no record of those workers."[158] By August 2011, TEPCO was reporting that the whereabouts

DOI: 10.1057/9781137343123

of 143 workers was unknown.[159] TEPCO also reported in August that a 40-year-old worker died of acute leukemia after working at the plant for seven days.[160] In July 2012, it was revealed that a subcontractor at the Fukushima plant had required workers to blanket their personal radiation detection devices in lead in an effort to keep their official radiation exposure under the safety threshold.[161] In November 2012, *The Asahi Shimbun* reported that workers involved in the disaster cleanup were not being given the special allowance of between 3,300 yen and 10,000 yen allocated by the Environment Ministry for workers in radiation contaminated areas. The article implied that the six general contractors were withholding the allowances. *The Asahi Shimbun* noted that it had found instances of nonpayment in all six projects of 100 million yen each.[162]

Concerns about the risks posed to workers continued to be reported in the Japanese media through the end of 2012. In December 2012, *The Asahi Shimbun* interviewed workers who claim that TEPCO assigned contractors to the highest radiation areas and that these contractors feared for their health but were driven by economic imperatives to take these dangerous jobs: "Workers come from around the country because they are willing to work even at a nuclear plant due to the economic slump," one worker said.[163] He continued: "Many businesses siphon off part of their wages, taking advantage of their vulnerable positions." Another worker in his 20s who was interviewed asserted "I was told to work at the plant like a kamikaze pilot…I have no idea about how much radiation I was exposed to." The worker expressed concern for his future health and ability to produce healthy children. Unfortunately, the Japanese government's difficulties in keeping track of contract workers and its decision to restrict cancer surveys for workers[164] may ultimately privatize the risks for health impacts when sickened former plant workers lack formal documentation of their time spent at the plant and/or their levels of radiation exposure.

Ocean contamination

Consensus holds that Fukushima constitutes the greatest radiological release into the ocean ever to occur. According to Woods Hole Oceanographic Institution in Massachusetts, levels of radioactive cesium reached more than 100,000 Becquerels per cubic meter in early April 2011.[165] The French Institute for Radiological Protection and Nuclear Safety (IRSN) described Fukushima as the world's worst nuclear

DOI: 10.1057/9781137343123

contamination event ever for the ocean, reporting that from 21 March to 27 July, 27.1 petabecquerels (PBq) of Cesium-137 contaminated the ocean.[166] Other estimates range up to 34P Bq.[167] One PBq is equivalent to a million billion Becquerels, or 10^15.[168] Few figures are available for radioisotopes other than Cesium-134, Cesium-137 and Strontium-90.

The ocean was contaminated by Fukushima Daiichi in several ways. First, most of the radiation lofted into the atmosphere by the March explosions fell out over the Pacific Ocean. Second, additional contamination occurred as water used to cool the site during the early days of the disaster poured directly into the ocean. On 2 April 2011, Masao Yoshida, then plant manager at Daiichi, confirmed that highly radioactive liquid was flowing from reactor 2 into the ocean: "We have confirmed a worst-case situation. Water containing extremely high levels of radiation is flowing into the sea."[169] He estimated that the level of radioactivity in the water flowing into the sea exceeded 1,000 millisieverts.[170] Third, radiation contamination of the Pacific persisted as the Daiichi site saturation by water challenged all efforts at capture, containment, and decontamination.

TEPCO admitted in May 2013 that the reactor buildings 1–3 will require years of continuous water injections to prevent nuclear fires from erupting.[171] TEPCO quantified injections in May 2013 at 400 tons daily. The volume of water required for cooling has risen across time. In October 2011, TEPCO stated that approximately 70 tons of water was sprayed around the Daiichi compound daily.[172] In September 012, TEPCO reported water injections were five tons per hour at unit 1 reactor; seven tons per hour at unit 2; seven tons per hour at unit 3.[173] Capturing and decontaminating water used in injections has been extraordinarily challenging given the structural damage to the reactor buildings.

Ground water seepage has also contributed to the volume of radioactive water requiring capture, decontamination and storage in the buildings. TEPCO announced in April 2013 that 400 tons of ground water flowed into the reactor buildings daily, in addition to the water produced by deliberate injections.[174] The site saturation may also contaminate fresh water aquifers. *Al Jazeera* reported in October 2012 that nuclear engineer and college lecturer Masashi Goto is concerned that radioactive water in Daiichi's reactor basements may be contaminating the underground water system, potentially traveling long distances to threaten public water supplies.[175]

Storage of the contaminated water that is successfully captured at the site has been an ongoing problem. The World Nuclear Association

DOI: 10.1057/9781137343123

reported that by the end of March 2011, all water storage tanks – the condenser units and condensate tanks – around units 1 through 4 were full of contaminated water pumped from the buildings.[176] TEPCO improvised by importing large water storage units, which were situated and filled around the Daiichi site. Eventually, huge pools were excavated at the site and lined for storing contaminated water. By May 2013 *The Asahi Shimbun* reported the Daiichi site held approximately 280,000 tons of radioactive water, while an additional 100,000 tons were believed to reside in the basements of units 1 through 4, as well as in the turbine buildings.[177] Leakage of contaminated water from these pools poses an ongoing problem.[178] By the spring of 2013 TEPCO was running out of storage.[179]

TEPCO has been struggling to decontaminate the water in its storage tanks. A wastewater treatment facility was built early in the disaster, but the various decontamination systems implemented have been unable to eliminate all radionuclides, especially tritium.[180] Filtered water was reported as measuring 710 million Becquerels per liter while unfiltered water was reported as twice as radioactive in May 2013.[181] Tritium was believed to the major source of residual contamination in the filtered water.[182] The filtration system has accidentally dumped unfiltered water, contaminated with Cesium-134, Cesium-137, and Iodine-131, into the sea.[183]

Ken Buesseler, a scientist at Woods Hole Oceanography Institute, has been very public about his concerns for the ocean. In a research publication with M. Aoyama, and M. Fukasawa, Buesseler reported that Fukushima Cesium-137 radiation in the sea near the plant peaked in April 2011 at 50 million times above normal levels.[184] In a separate interview with *Straight* on 28 October 2011, Buesseler stated that Fukushima was by far the greatest accidental release of radiation into ocean waters, the magnitude of which in April 2011 was over 100 times of Chernobyl's contamination of the Black Sea.[185] Buesseler observed in October 2012 that "the nuclear power plants continue to leak radioactive contamination into the ocean."[186] TEPCO's own data support Buesseler's observations: TEPCO reported that radioactive Cesium-134 density actually increased in September of 2012 around the discharge channels of units 5 and 6 as compared to April 2012.[187]

Ongoing and persistent radiation contamination poses long-term risks to the ecosystem. On 26 October 2012, *The Asahi Shimbun* reported that cesium levels in fish off the coast of Fukushima were not dropping. The article addressed an email from Hideo Yamazaki,

DOI: 10.1057/9781137343123

a marine biologist at Kinki University, asserting the plant would continue to contaminate the ocean for years until massive structural repairs occurred at the site: "The current levels of contamination in the fish and seafood from the Fukushima coast will continue for a while, perhaps more than 10 years, judging from the progress in the cleanup process."[188] Marine animals at the top of the food chain and birds that feed on marine life will become highly contaminated under these conditions. In August 2012, *Jiji Press* reported that "25,800 Becquerels of Cesium Detected in Fish Caught off Fukushima."[189] In March 2013, a fish measuring 740,000 Bq/kg was caught off Fukushima.[190] In April 2012 the Japanese media reported: "Cesium up to 100 times levels before disaster found in plankton far off nuke plant."[191]

Widespread dispersion of Fukushima radioisotopes in the ocean was confirmed by Japanese scientists who had found radiocesium in plankton at ten locations, ranging from Hokkaido Japan to Guam between January and February of 2012.[192] Other research findings corroborate findings of wide dispersion of Fukushima radioisotopes. A study published in *Environmental Science Technology* in 2012 reported that radiostrontium levels in surface seawater remain elevated and were in some areas comparable, to or even higher, than those measured for Cesium-137 in December 2011.[193] The researchers concluded that the total amount of Strontium 90 released into the marine environment could reach approximately 1 PBq. A separate study estimated that direct discharges of Strontium 90 range between 90 and 900 TeraBq.[194] Yet another study found Cesium-134 deposits in marine snow gathered 2,000 kilometers away from the plant at depths of 5,000 meters measuring 1,200 Bq/kg.[195]

Contamination has been detected as far away as U.S. coastal waters in Southern California. A third study, focusing on radioiodine in U.S. coastal kelp, reported that a high of 40 MBq 131I, or 40,000,000 Bq/kg of Iodine-131 had been detected in one bed of Macrocystis Pyrifera off the coast of Southern California in the summer of 2011.[196] The researchers of the kelp study described their findings in a local Long Beach media interview:

> "Radioactivity is taken up by the kelp and anything that feeds on the kelp will be exposed to this also," [California State University, Long Beach

DOI: 10.1057/9781137343123

marine biology professors Steven L. Manley] continued. "Even though we detected low levels, it still got into the environment and we don't know anything about the other radioisotopes like Cesium 137, which stays around much longer than iodine. In fact, the values that we reported for iodine probably underestimate what was probably in there. It could be two to three times more because we were just sampling the surface tissue; the biomass estimates were based on canopy tissue and a lot of kelp biomass is underneath. So, probably two or three times more was in the tissue at its height. Then it enters the coastal food web and gets dispersed over a variety of organisms. I would assume it's there. It's not a good thing, but whether it actually has a measureable [sic] detrimental effect is beyond my expertise."[197]

Kelp and plankton are at the bottom of the food chain. The radioisotopes in kelp will bio-magnify up the food chain.

Predicting long-term environmental and health effects is complicated by uncertainties about the "fallout" levels of various radioisotopes. How long will the radioisotopes inflict damage on the environment? A study modeling dilution declines of Cesium-137 published in *Environmental Research Letters* predicted that after seven years the "total peak radioactivity levels would still be about twice the pre-Fukushima values off the coastal waters of North America"[198] However, the persistent nature of some radioisotopes, such as Cesium-137 and Plutonium-239, facilitate bio-accumulation within a species, and bio-magnification across species over years. For example, tritium bio-accumulates in phytoplankton and bio-magnifies up the food chain into mussels, thereby posing a persistent and toxic contaminant with intergenerational effects.[199]

The oceans were in "shocking decline" prior to the Fukushima disaster.[200] A research article studying the geological record on ocean acidification found that no past event in the 300-million-year record matches future projections of disruptions to the balance of ocean carbonate chemistry.[201] The ongoing releases of contaminated water into the Pacific may have tremendous adverse consequences for an already stressed ecosystem. Furthermore, contaminants in the ocean do not necessarily stay in the ocean. The cycle of contamination is not limited to land animals consuming ocean life. Contaminants in the ocean – including heavy substances such as mercury – are known to enter the atmosphere directly from the ocean.[202]

DOI: 10.1057/9781137343123

Fallout in North America

What about populations in the United States exposed to Fukushima fallout? President Obama went on record on 7 March 2011 declaring to U.S. citizens that they faced no risk of significant radiation fallout in the United States.[203] NRC Chairman Gregory Jaczko was quoted in *The Wall Street Journal* on 15 March 2011 as asserting it was "very unlikely" that harmful levels of radiation would reach the United States: "You just aren't going to have any radiological material that, by the time it traveled those large distances, could present any risk to the American public."[204] Meanwhile, President Obama reaffirmed his support of nuclear power.[205]

Despite assurances, radioactive fallout occurred in the United States beginning in mid-March. By 29 March "traces of radiation from the crippled nuclear plant in Japan" were reported as being detected in states from California to Massachusetts but "state officials say there is no public-health risk."[206] Japanese simulations estimated that radioactive dust was lifted high in the atmosphere over Japan on 14 and 15 March by updrafts and reached the United States via the jet stream by 17–18 March.[207] As explained above, the use of salt water on the hot fuel may have increased transportability of uranium. Professor Watanabe, of Fukushima University, reported in September 2012 that a radioactive atmospheric plume was circling the earth every 40 days, with fallout still showing spikes.[208] Fallout dispersion would be affected by the jet stream and local weather and topographical conditions.

The assertion of no public health risk echoed in media accounts across the United States and Canada, despite levels of Iodine-131 300 times current background levels reported in March in British Columbia.[209] Air filter analyses conducted by scientists in Washington State were made public in June 2011 by Arnie Gundersen in an interview with Chris Martenson. Gundersen claimed that independent scientists located in Seattle found high amounts of "hot" particles of cesium, strontium, plutonium, uranium, and Cobalt-60. Their data analysis indicated that U.S. citizens in Seattle breathed in on average five hot particles a day in April (citizens in Tokyo inhaled approximately ten a day and those in Fukushima prefecture over 30 times that amount).[210] Hot particles lodge in bodily tissues and emit radiation as they decay. In the right circumstances, one hot particle can cause cancer.

Scientific findings of high levels of noble gases in the United States lend support to Gundersen's data. In June 2012, researchers from the

DOI: 10.1057/9781137343123

Pacific Northwest National Laboratory and the University of Texas published for public review a power point presentation titled "US Particulate and Xenon Measurements Made Following the Fukushima Reactor Accident".[211] The researchers had used a SAUNA-II xenon measurement system in March and April 2011 to measure noble gases from Fukushima reaching the U.S. Pacific Northwest. The system measured Xenon-133 at 450,000 times background. The levels persisted for weeks. Xenon-133 emits beta particles (high intensity electrons) and gamma rays as it decays. Inhalation of Xenon poses a danger to human health.

The U.S. EPA Radnet system tasked with air monitoring failed. The EPA Office of the Inspector General issued a report in 2012 that noted 20 percent of the EPA's stationary radiation monitors were not functioning at the time of the Fukushima accident.[212] Additionally, other monitors had not had their filters changed and were therefore not able to provide accurate readings. The Inspector General report concluded that the EPA Radnet system had "relaxed quality controls."

The declassified NRC transcripts of conference calls that occurred on 17 March 2011 reveal that the agency had projections of a 40 millisievert dose to the thyroid from radioactive iodine alone for a one-year old child in California: "The DITTRA result was four rem [40,000 microsieverts or 40 millisieverts] to the thyroid of a one year-old child based on one year integration of uptake."[213] Parents in North America were not warned about the dangers of radioactive iodine in dairy products. In the spring of 2013, the Obama Administration approved dramatic increases in radiation exposure limits allowable under EPA protective action guidelines used in nuclear disasters.[214]

There have been two published studies so far in U.S. academic journals on the relationship between Fukushima fallout rates and U.S. health risks. Janet Sherman and Joseph Mangano reported in 2012 a 35 percent spike in infant mortality rates for the ten weeks following Fukushima's March releases in eight U.S. cities (Boise ID, Seattle WA, Portland OR, plus the northern California cities of Santa Cruz, Sacramento, San Francisco, San Jose, and Berkeley).[215] The study's conclusions were publicly debated.[216] In 2013, Mangano and Sherman published findings from a second study suggesting radiation exposure could be linked to increased incidences of congenital hypothyroid cases in West Coast newborns.[217] They correlated elevated airborne beta levels in the Pacific/West Coast U.S. states with hypothyroidism in newborns. They found that the number of congenital hypothyroid cases in Alaska, California,

DOI: 10.1057/9781137343123

Hawaii, Oregon, and Washington in the period ranging from 17 March to 31 December 2011 was 16 percent greater than for the same period in 2010. This finding compared to a 3 percent decline in 36 other U.S. States. A 28 percent divergence between the Pacific/West Coast states and the 36 others occurred in the period March 17–June 30 (p < 0.04).

Public concern and debate about the risks of fallout in the United States and elsewhere may have been tempered by carefully orchestrated communication campaigns. "No health effects are expected among the Japanese people as a result of the events at Fukushima," read a statement issued by the Nuclear Energy Institute, a nuclear industry trade group, at a June Washington press conference.[218] According to *The Guardian*, two days after the earthquake, British government authorities contacted nuclear companies – including Westinghouse, Areva, EDF Energy, and the Nuclear Industry Association – to coordinate a public relations campaign assuring nuclear safety, in order to prevent resistance to a new generation of planned nuclear plants for the United Kingdom.[219] In April, the U.K. office for nuclear development met with nuclear companies in London "to discuss a joint communications and engagement strategy aimed at ensuring we maintain confidence among the British public on the safety of nuclear power stations and nuclear new-build policy in light of recent events at the Fukushima nuclear power plant." Institutional collusion between government and the nuclear industry is a historic phenomenon rooted in the Cold War, as explained in Chapter 2.

Ongoing fallout fears in Japan

As noted previously, Keinichi Ohmae, president of BBT University, had asserted in his "Lessons from Fukushima Dai-ichi" report that 14 nuclear reactors in Japan were extensively damaged by the earthquake, although the report did not detail the specific damage.[220] Did any other plants release radiation after the March earthquake? One plant that stands out is the Fukushima Daini plant, located ten kilometers away from Daiichi. On 5 May 2011, IAEA Deputy Director General and Head of Department of Nuclear Safety and Security, Denis Flory reported that as of 21 April, the exclusion zone around Fukushima Daini plant was reduced from ten kilometers to eight kilometers.[221] The basis for the establishment of the exclusion zone in March 2011 was ambiguous. In July 2012, *The Wall Street Journal* reported that rising background radiation levels at

DOI: 10.1057/9781137343123

the Daini plant, which had risen to 0.5 to 1.0 microsieverts per hour, threatened long-term efforts to continue stabilization of Fukushima Daini's reactors.[222] Problems were also reported for the Tokai nuclear plant. In October 2011, Japan Atomic Power stated that repairs to Tokai Daini reactor would take nine months longer than planned.[223] Reports of fires and radiological water spills at the reactors in Tokai in the winter of 2011/2012 lent support to concerns about the possibility of radiation releases from other reactors in Japan.[224]

It appears, however, that the greatest visible risk remains the Fukushima Daiichi plant. Scientific evidence indicates fallout is already bio-accumulating in animal life. The risks for people are indeterminate. Furthermore, although exact figures for total atmospheric and ocean releases are not known, it is clear that the disaster is not yet over as the plant continues to emit radiation daily into the atmosphere and ocean. Exacerbating risks are the plant conditions. The plant infrastructure has not been stabilized and is regarded as highly vulnerable to further earthquakes and/or ground subsistence from water absorption.

Watchers of the TEPCO and TBS-JNN webcams trained on Fukushima observed that massive steam and smoke releases began at the plant around 1 May 2012 and worsening again in June 2013.[225] TEPCO estimated in July 2012 that ten million Becquerels of radioactive material per hour were still being released into the atmosphere from the plant's airborne emissions.[226] The true extent of accumulating fallout throughout Japan and elsewhere, particularly North America, remains unclear. Studies have been conducted in selected areas of fallout, but the uneven and often unpredictable patterns of radiation fallout complicate extrapolations. What is even less clear is the extent to which animal life has taken in radioisotopes through inhalation and ingestion. Inhalation risks are greatest during the fallout peak. However, risks from ingestion continue over years because radio-isotopes bio-accumulate and bio-magnify across species.

Four studies published in late 2012 raised concern about the potential health impacts of the disaster based on empirical observations of animal exposure in the Fukushima Prefecture. The first study, addressing bio-accumulation of cesium in Japanese macaques, was conducted by researchers, Shunsuke Kimura and Akira Hatano, from Nippon Veterinary and Life Science University (NVLU).[227] The researchers found that concentrations in the macaques flesh ranged between 10,000 and 25,000 Bk/kg, in the immediate wake of the crisis on 2011. The readings then fell to 500–1,500 Bk/kg in June 2011, but rose again to more than

DOI: 10.1057/9781137343123

2,000 Bk/kg in the spring of 2012. The researchers believe that consumption of leaf buds explain the seasonal variation because leaf buds will have higher levels of cesium, a potassium analog. Research on rodent populations in Belarus after the Chernobyl accident found that maximum levels of radiocesium from this disaster peaked one to two years after deposition while concentrations of Strontium 90 increased up to the tenth year.[228] Americium241, a transuranic element, was not detected for five years, but then increased up to the tenth year with an expected increase in the future.

The second study examined the "abundance of birds in Fukushima as judged from Chernobyl."[229] The study notes that previous research has established a negative relationship between animal abundance and radiation. The researchers tested this relationship using breeding bird census data collected in Chernobyl from 2006 to 2009 and in Fukushima in 2011, focusing on 14 bird species found in both regions. The researchers found a strongly negative relationship between animal abundance and radiation in both regions, but the relationship was more pronounced in Fukushima. The researchers offered several potential explanations for the more strongly negative relationship in Fukushima, including the possibility that composition of radionuclides found in Fukushima were more dangerous for birds. However, what is important about this study is the demonstration that bird populations within Fukushima were immediately and significantly adversely impacted by their exposure to radiation.

A third study on Fukushima effects examined radiation's biological impacts on the pale grass blue butterfly.[230] The researchers collected 144 adult samples from ten different locations in May 2011 and again in September 2011. A 12.4 percent abnormality rate was found in field-caught butterflies from May 2011. Abnormalities in forewing size were detected in field-caught butterflies from higher radiation areas. The researchers found that the male forewing size was negatively correlated with ground radiation levels at the collections sites. Results also included an increase in mutations in leg appendages and antennae correlated positively with collections sites with higher levels of radiation. The researchers bred the butterflies and found *substantially increased mutation rates among offspring generations*, an approximate tripling of the overall abnormality rate by generation two. The researchers compared mutations in their lab-bred butterflies with mutations in 238 butterflies collected from the field in September and early October 2011. The butterflies collected in the fall

DOI: 10.1057/9781137343123

of 2011 exhibited 28.1 percent mutations, double the rate observed in the field-collected butterflies from May 2011 with a mutation rate of 60.2 percent for the first generation offspring of the fall field-caught butterflies. The mutation rates across generations are alarming because, as the lead researcher Joji Otaki from the University of Ryukus, Okinawa told BBC on 13 August 2012: "It had been believed that insects are very resistant to radiation... In that sense, our results were unexpected."[231]

The study was criticized for focusing on a butterfly known to migrate, but a significant finding remains uncontested, that is the increased rate of mutations across generations after exposure to radiation compared to controls. The mutations and the genome instability found in the butterfly study echo findings of a study of voles published in 2006 by Ryabokon and Goncharova, "Transgenerational Accumulation of Radiation in Small Mammals Chronically Exposed to Chernobyl Fallout."[232] The researchers followed 22 generations of voles over ten years. A main finding of "long term development of biological damage under low dose rate irradiation" was "permanently elevated levels of chromosome aberrations and an increasing frequency of embryonic lethality." The researchers concluded that radiation exposure to parental generations led to an "accumulated pool of germline mutations and/or epigenetic changes, which resulted in the observed, persistently elevated levels of chromosome aberrations in somatic cells and an increase in embryonic losses in later generations." Moller and Mousseau concluded in a 2006 review of research that levels of mutations in a wide range of plants and animals around Chernobyl ranges from 2 to 20 times normal levels, depending upon the affected species.[233]

The fourth study titled, "Differences in Effects of Radiation on Abundance of Animals in Fukushima and Chernobyl" published in 2013 analyzed and compared counts and conditions of spiders, grasshoppers, dragonflies, butterflies, bumblebees, cicadas, and birds at 1,198 sites in the Chernobyl and Fukushima Daiichi regions.[234] The study found that all taxa of animals suffered significant declines in abundance in Chernobyl (now 25 years since the accident). The study's data for Fukushima, collected six months after the accident, indicated significant declines in abundance of birds, butterflies, and cicadas, but not yet in bumblebees, dragonflies, and grasshoppers. The researchers concluded from the Chernobyl data that population declines increase over years of chronic exposure because of the long-term effects of mutation accumulation.

DOI: 10.1057/9781137343123

The Japanese government has announced that it plans to study human genetic effects from the Fukushima disaster.[235] However, detection of genetic effects happens after damage has occurred. Even life-shortening consequences, such as cancer, typically take years to be expressed in the absence of acute exposure. The full effects will unfold across generations. Thus, the value in the research will be derived from its *retrospective* empirical confirmation that exposure to radioisotopes through inhalation and ingestion affect health and development.

Risks for present populations within Fukushima and elsewhere could magnify if the Fukushima plant infrastructures collapse further. In the spring of 2012, prominent figures in Japan warned the plant's collapsing infrastructure threatened more significant releases, particularly a collapse of unit 4 spent fuel pool. Former Japanese UN diplomat Akio Matsumura posted a letter to the UN authored by Mr. Mitsuhei Murata, Japan's former ambassador to Switzerland, on his (Matsumura's) webpage with this explanation:

> Japan's former Ambassador to Switzerland, Mr. Mitsuhei Murata, was invited to speak at the Public Hearing of the Budgetary Committee of the House of Councilors on March 22, 2012, on the Fukushima nuclear power plants accident. Before the Committee, Ambassador Murata strongly stated that if the crippled building of reactor unit 4 – with 1,535 fuel rods in the spent fuel pool 100 feet (30 meters) above the ground – collapses, not only will it cause a shutdown of all six reactors but will also affect the common spent fuel pool containing 6,375 fuel rods, located some 50 meters from reactor 4. In both cases the radioactive rods are not protected by a containment vessel; dangerously, they are open to the air. This would certainly cause a global catastrophe like we have never before experienced. He stressed that the responsibility of Japan to the rest of the world is immeasurable. Such a catastrophe would affect us all for centuries. Ambassador Murata informed us that the total numbers of the spent fuel rods at the Fukushima Daiichi site excluding the rods in the pressure vessel is 11,421 (396 + 615 + 566 + 1,535 + 994 + 940 + 6,375).[236]

Mitsushei Murata's letter dated 25 March 2012 to Secretary General Honorable Ban Ki-moon specifically addresses the threat to Japan and "the whole world" posed by NO. 4 reactor":

> I was asked to make a statement at the public hearing of the Budgetary Committee of the House of Councilors on March 23. I raised the crucial problem of No.4 reactor of Fukushima containing 1535 fuel rods. It could be fatally damaged by continuing aftershocks. Moreover, 50 meters away from

DOI: 10.1057/9781137343123

it exists a common cooling pool for 6 reactors containing 6375 fuel rods! It is no exaggeration to say that the fate of Japan and the whole world depends on NO.4 reactor. This is confirmed by most reliable experts like Dr. Arnie Gundersen or Dr. Fumiaki Koide.

Any response to the letter was not made publicly available. On 1 May 2012, a coalition of Japanese civil organizations sent a second letter to the UN Secretary General pleading for assistance:

> We Japanese civil organizations express our deepest concern that our government does not inform its citizens about the extent of risk of the Fukushima Daiichi Unit 4 spent nuclear fuel pool. Given the fact that collapse of this pool could potentially lead to catastrophic consequences with worldwide implications, what the Japanese government should be doing as a responsible member of the international community is to avoid any further disaster by mobilizing all the wisdom and the means available in order to stabilize this spent nuclear fuel. It is clearly evident that Fukushima Daiichi Unit 4 spent nuclear fuel pool is no longer a Japanese issue but an international issue with potentially serious consequences. Therefore, it is imperative for the Japanese government and the international community to work together on this crisis before it becomes too late. We are appealing to the United Nations to help Japan and the planet in order to prevent the irreversible consequences of a catastrophe that could affect generations to come. We herewith make our urgent request to you as follows:
>
> 1   The United Nations should organize a Nuclear Security Summit to take up the crucial problem of the Fukushima Daiichi Unit 4 spent nuclear fuel pool.
> 2   The United Nations should establish an independent assessment team on Fukushima Daiichi Unit 4 and coordinate international assistance in order to stabilize the unit's spent nuclear fuel and prevent radiological consequences with potentially catastrophic consequences.[217]

What conditions at the plant warranted such desperate pleas for assistance? Akio Matsumura included on his web-posting comments made by Robert Alvarez regarding the amount of fuel stored at Fukushima Daiichi:

> Based on U.S. Energy Department data, assuming a total of 11,138 spent fuel assemblies are being stored at the Dai-Ichi site, nearly all of which is in pools. They contain roughly 336 million curies (~1.2 E+19 Bq) of long-lived radioactivity. About 134 million curies is Cesium-137 – roughly 85 times the amount of Cs-137 released at the Chernobyl accident as estimated by

the U.S. National Council on Radiation Protection (NCRP). The total spent reactor fuel inventory at the Fukushima-Daiichi site contains nearly half of the total amount of Cs-137 estimated by the NCRP to have been released by all atmospheric nuclear weapons testing, Chernobyl, and world-wide reprocessing plants (~270 million curies or ~9.9 E+18 Becquerel).[238]

Alvarez's figure for the total amount of radiation contained in the fuel inventory at Fukushima is sobering: nearly half of the total amount of Cesium-137 estimated to have been released by all atmospheric testing, Chernobyl, and worldwide reprocessing plants.

In April 2013, Akio Matsumura declared "the crisis not over" in a letter he wrote and issued publicly to UN Secretary General Ban Ki-moon.[239] In this letter, Matsumura explained that "radioactively polluted water is leaking out of the plants and that the site is in a new state of emergency" and that "the mechanism that stands between safety and a fire at the Fukushima Daiichi plant is, to say the least, precarious." He observes that the attention afforded to the disaster has been marginal given "the situation is still relegated to the back pages of our papers, and thus to the back of our leaders' minds."

Murata and Matsumura have not been alone in their efforts to bring attention to the disaster and its incalculable risks. A wide variety of Japanese citizens have agitated for a more concerted international response to stabilize the plant. One group mentioned previously in this chapter is the Skilled Veterans Corps for Fukushima. This group includes over 700 Japanese citizens skilled in the areas of engineering and technology. Their founder, Yastel Yamada, travelled to the United States and was interviewed on 30 July 2012 in Ukia, CA by TUC radio concerning their desire to gain access to and help stabilize the Fukushima plant. TEPCO has forbidden their access.[240] It was in his presentation in California that Mr. Yamada reported that the fuel from the Fukushima reactors could be in powder form.

Still others from Japan have also attempted to raise awareness of the risks posed by the disaster. On 4 May 2012 a forum with Japanese medical and nuclear experts was held in New York City. It was broadcasted at the website, *Cinema Forum Fukushima*, titled, "Archive Footage of the NYC Press Conference May 4th 2012." One of the speakers was Dr. Junro Fuse, Internist and head of Kosugi Medical Clinic near Tokyo, Japan.[241] Dr. Fuse argued that information about contaminated hot spots was being "restricted" in Japan by the Ministry on Education, Culture, Sports, Science and Technology. He also claimed that symptoms of exposure to

DOI: 10.1057/9781137343123

internal emitters were occurring in Tokyo. He asserted that exposure to internal radiation through the accidental ingestion of radioisotopes is 200 to 600 times more damaging than exposure to external radiation, but few doctors and academics in Japan have knowledge or training regarding their detection or effects.

Professor Hiroaki Koide, Nuclear Reactor Specialist and Assistant Professor at Kyoto University Research Reactor Institute, also spoke at the conference.[242] Professor Koide discussed the amount of radiation released in March 2011 and the status of the reactors at the plant. He stated that the Japanese government report submitted to the IAEA quantified the radiation released by the explosions of March 2011 at 15,000 terabecquerels of Cesium-137 alone. This figure did not include other radioisotopes, nor did it include ocean contamination. Yet, this figure amounts to 170 times the amount of Cesium-137 released by the Hiroshima explosion (Hiroshima was 89 terabecquerels of Cesium-137).

Professor Koide went on to explain that three of the other reactors at the plant, reactors 1, 2, and 3, all had core meltdowns and the current locations of the melted fuel rods are unknown. He noted that significant releases of radiation contamination continue into the ocean. Professor Koide concluded that humanity as a whole has never experienced this level of radiation contamination and he stated "I have no idea what will happen but we will be fighting this radiation on the order of tens, hundreds of years."

Risk, accountability, and responsibility

How do people at risk respond when the risks are incalculable? Environmental lawsuits require evidence of destruction of property and/or physical harm to person and so they tend to occur years after the injury was first incurred. Proving harm to self and property requires establishing that contamination levels pose unacceptable risks to health across time. This can be a challenging task for claimants when effects may take years, if not generations, to unfold. Despite challenges, citizens in Japan have through advocacy and legal suits sought to mitigate Fukushima risks. Their efforts have often been met with privatizing responses.

During the early days of the disaster outraged citizens in Fukushima Prefecture met with TEPCO and Japanese government officials demanding that decontamination and evacuation provisions be extended

DOI: 10.1057/9781137343123

further. Citizens were particularly upset that the government's permissible exposure level was raised to 20 millisieverts. One 19 July meeting between citizens and Japanese government officials was immortalized on YouTube.[243] During the YouTube video of the event, a spokesperson for the people of Fukushima repeatedly asks, "As other people do, people in Fukushima have a right to avoid the radiation exposure and live a healthy life, too. Don't you think so?"

The government official, Akira Satoh, Director of the Local Nuclear Emergency Response Headquarters, responds, "The government has tried to reduce the radiation exposure dose as much as it can."

The citizens' spokesperson presses, "So, are you saying that they don't? They have that right, don't they?"

The government official identified as Mr. Satoh, responds, "I don't know if they have that right."

The spokesperson then queries, "Do you mean that there is a difference in the radiation exposure standards between Fukushima prefecture and other prefectures?"

The official, responds, "What I am saying is, the government has tried to reduce the radiation exposure dose as much as it can."

The audience reacts, disgruntled by the evasiveness and their spokesperson again presses, "The government isn't applying a different standard to people in Fukushima, is it?"

The official concludes tersely, "I have already said all I could say" and left, amidst cries from the audience that they wanted their children's urine tested for radioactivity. The audience demanded also to know why the Soviets were able to evacuate over 200,000 children within two weeks of the disaster yet Japan, a "free society," failed to protect its citizenry. There were no answers from the departing officials.

In June 2012, 1,324 Fukushima citizens filed a criminal complaint against TEPCO and the Japanese government.[244] The complaint named 33 TEPCO executives and the Japanese government's Nuclear Safety Commission:

> The commission is accused of negligence in regard to its responsibility to take adequate safety precautions at the Fukushima plant. In the aftermath of the devastating earthquake and tsunami, the failure on the part of the named executives to ensure the plant's safety led to the meltdown, the complaint says. Furthermore, it claims the meltdown and the delay in releasing information about the scale of the radiation leakage exposed residents to

radioactive materials, caused injury and emotional damages, and even provoked suicides.

Few options exist for the citizens of Fukushima other than litigation. Allegations that TEPCO intended to "abandon" the Fukushima Daiichi nuclear plant on 14 and 15 March 2011 and "evacuate" the Fukushima Daini plant due to high radiation may provide support for the claimants' allegations of negligence.[245]

Litigation will require that Fukushima victims prove harm to their person and/or property. Proof of health injuries is particularly challenging for claimants. Linking exposure to disease in the absence of verified symptoms of acute exposure is a tentative and probabilistic enterprise, easily subject to dispute. For instance, in September 2012 the Fukushima Prefectural government announced its results from thyroid tests of about 80,000 children in Fukushima Prefecture.[246] As reported, the results indicated "no direct effects," although 425 children were found to have lumps of 5.1 millimeters or larger or cysts of 2.1 centimeters or larger. One child was found to have thyroid cancer and 27 were diagnosed with benign tumors. By June 2013, 12 Fukushima children were confirmed to have thyroid cancer.[247] Yet, researchers said the cancers could not be directly linked to the Fukushima disaster based on the amount of time that had elapsed since exposure. Data from Chernobyl suggest that thyroid cancer typically developed after four years of exposure. Proving harm in the years immediately after the disaster will be difficult given epidemiological evidence of harm takes years to accumulate.

Claimants must also establish the nature of TEPCO's legal liability, which has been subject to dispute. In 2011, TEPCO declared it had no legal liability for property damage due to radioactive fallout from the plant when taken to court by two golf course operators.[248] TEPCO asserted in court that "Radioactive materials (such as cesium) that scattered and fell from the Fukushima No. 1 nuclear plant belong to individual landowners there, not TEPCO." TEPCO also disputed the golf operators' measurements of the levels of contamination found on the course. The Tokyo District Court disagreed with TEPCO's claim of no liability, but the court assigned the responsibility for decontamination work to the central or local governments and it rejected the demand for compensation because the radiation levels were purportedly lower than 3.8 microsieverts an hour, which was the allowable limit set by the sci-

DOI: 10.1057/9781137343123

ence ministry for schoolyards. (3.8 microsieverts an hour equals 33.288 millisieverts a year.)

TEPCO has some liability for nuclear disasters under Japan's third-party liability legislation, the Act on Compensation for Nuclear Damage. However, as explained by Ximena Vasquez-Maignan, Senior Legal Adviser at the Legal Affairs Section of the OECD Nuclear Energy Agency, there are significant ambiguities in the law.[249] First, the law does not define the nature of the damage that must be compensated by the operator so the Japanese courts will have to make the final decision on what counts as nuclear damage. The courts will have to distinguish between damages directly caused by radiation and those caused by the earthquake and tsunami. TEPCO could actually be exonerated given the scale of the earthquake and tsunami. Another limit on litigation is the time frame. As explained by Vasquez-Maignan: "All rights of action are fully extinguished 20 years following the date of the tort and the actions must be brought within three years from the date at which the person suffering damage had knowledge both of the damage and of the person liable." Finally, TEPCO's financial liability may be unlimited in principle, but in practice the Japanese National Diet will offer financial support when TEPCO's liability exceeds JPY 120 billion through the legal auspices of the Facilitation Corporation, established by the Japanese Diet with the approval of the 3 August 2011 bill titled, "Establishment of a Nuclear Damage Compensation Facilitation Corporation." In the wake of the Tokai-mura nuclear accident in 1999, most claims were settled out of court.

Vasquez-Maignan interpreted the act as dictating that legal actions must be brought within three years of confirmation of harm to person and/or property. However, in January 2013 the blogger EX-SKF translated details of the proposed compensation statute of limitations:

> TEPCO and the Nuclear Damage Liability Facilitation Fund have decided that the period to claim damages from the Fukushima I Nuclear Power Plant accident will be three years from the date when people affected by the accident receive their application documents. It has been pointed out that the three-year statute of limitations from the start of the accident may happen, but the new plan will move the date further back from which to count three years so that people affected by the accident are able to receive compensations.[250]

According to EX-SKF, the plan is "part of the change request for the 'Comprehensive Special Business Plan' that TEPCO submitted to

DOI: 10.1057/9781137343123

Toshimitsu Motegi, Minister of Economy, Trade and Industry, on January 15." The effect of this decision, if uncontested, is that Fukushima victims will have only a five-to-six year time span within which to sue for damages to property and person. This is a very narrow timeline when many diseases caused by radiation exposure take years to manifest.

TEPCO's ability to make good on any claims is a function of massive capital injections by the Japanese government, accompanied by public tax hikes. By early spring of 2012 TEPCO was essentially bankrupt. Japan's private lenders signaled they would provide loans to TEPCO on two conditions: raising power tariffs and restarting reactors.[251] In July 2012, the Japanese government made 1 trillion yen direct equity investment into TEPCO using tax payer funds, affording it a voting right in excess of 50 percent. Additionally, the government announced it would provide 2.5 trillion yen in compensation to victims rather than forcing TEPCO to go into bankruptcy and liquidate assets to pay for the disaster. TEPCO was allowed to increase electricity rates by 8.46 percent for household consumers and 14.9 percent for corporations, which effectively transfers the direct financial cost for paying for the disaster to rate holders, as well as citizens. The shareholders and creditors would walk away "unscathed," according to *The Asahi Shimbun*.[252] TEPCO's costs for stabilizing the reactors were estimated at 1 trillion yen. Decontamination costs were expected to be substantial but, as explained in the article, "specific locations, the volume of soil to be removed and other details have yet to be determined."

Concern exists throughout northern Japan that evacuations will remain limited, cleanup costs will be localized, and that victims will have little time to establish proof of harm. De-centralization of cleanup costs shifts risk to localities. Limited liability shifts risk to those who bear externalities. A short statute of limitations further accentuates risk shift. Risk shifts still more to citizens by aggressive efforts to reestablish nuclear operations in Japan.

Japan's government, then led by the Democratic Party of Japan, promised in February 2012 to limit reactor restarts to those deemed safe by IAEA stress tests. Antinuclear demonstrations reached 45,000 people in Tokyo outside the prime minister's office in June 2012 after the Oi reactor was restarted.[253] As explained in Chapter 2, the government responded by establishing the Nuclear Regulation Authority (NRA) in September 2012 to provide independent regulatory oversight.[254] However, the LDP, which was voted into power in December 2012, has aggressively pursued

DOI: 10.1057/9781137343123

pro-nuclear policies and pushed for quick reviews of reactor safety.[255] Nuclear is essential to the LDP security matrix, as illustrated by its efforts to ensure nuclear reprocessing processes at Rokkasho because of the "deterrent force it offers."[256]

The NRA's capacity to ensure nuclear safety remains unclear. NRA chairman Shunichi Tanaka stated in December 2012 that he could use "nonbinding administrative discretion" measures to order Kansai Electric Power Co. to close down operations at the Oi plant if a fault found there was determined to be active.[257] However, he acknowledged ambiguity existed regarding the legal force of its powers in probabilistic scenarios. For example, Tanaka explained that "it would be difficult to issue a legally binding shutdown order after the discovery of an active fault beneath an emergency water intake channel because that would be short of constituting imminent danger." The NRA's neutrality was called into question in February 2013 when the *Japan Times* reported that a high-level NRA officer had 30 illicit meetings with nuclear utilities.[258] Were utility profits prioritized over public safety?

The risks from a problem at the Rokkasho reprocessing facility are significant and have generated international attention.[259] Scientific review of the Rokkasho site determined the plant resides on an active fault.[260] Rokkasho currently stores 240 cubic meters of radioactive liquid waste that must be cooled continuously. An earthquake could disrupt cooling of that waste. The German nuclear industry calculated that an explosion at the Rokkasho facility could "expose persons within a 100 kilometer radius from the plant to radiation 10 to 100 times the lethal level, which presumably means instant death."[261] Despite these risks, the LDP remains firmly committed to the entire nuclear security complex.

In sum, policy responses to Fukushima illustrate the privatization of risk in several ways. First, risks for externalities from radiation contamination will be shouldered by the public. *The Asahi Shimbun* concluded in May 2013 that "the government avoided setting stringent radiation reference levels for the return of Fukushima evacuees for fear of triggering a population drain and being hit by ballooning costs for compensation, an *Asahi Shimbun* investigation shows." The move to raise permissible exposure levels clearly requires citizens to shoulder more risk. Second, economic risks have been shifted from TEPCO and its shareholders to the Japanese people more generally as the government raised taxes to pay for its bailout.[262] Future risk has also been transferred to the Japanese people as TEPCO and other nuclear utilities press for

DOI: 10.1057/9781137343123

permission to restart reactors idled for safety reviews within a timeline considered unreasonable by Japan's new nuclear regulator.

What health risks do Japanese citizens actually face? Will Fukushima children's right to health be compromised?[263] One of Japan's most vocal physicians, 95-year-old Shuntaro Hida, charged in the summer of 2012 that people in Japan were already starting to develop symptoms of internal radiation poisoning, including fatigue, diarrhea, and hair loss, resulting from the ingestion and/or inhalation of radioistopes.[264] Dr. Hida is a native of Hiroshima. After the bombing there he treated patients exposed to the fallout. In 1950 he opened a clinic to help those afflicted and stigmatized by their radiation illness. Hida told *The Japan Times*: "I am worried because I received such calls much earlier than I expected." He explained his concerns about censorship:

> Under the Occupation until the early 1950s, people were forbidden from "speaking, recording or doing research into symptoms of atomic-bomb survivors," he says. "I was stalked by the military police when I was talking about what I witnessed in Hiroshima," and arrested several times by the Occupation forces for "not abiding by their Occupation policy."

Hida asserted the United States "concealed" information about fallout-related illnesses in Japan and has since censored public knowledge and about research about exposure to ionizing radiation, particularly through internally ingested alpha and beta emitters.[265] History is repeating itself as the symptoms of radiation contamination in Japan are being hidden once again, he argued.

Fukushima fallout also poses potential health risks to non-Japanese citizens. In December 2012, eight crew members aboard the USS Ronald Reagan, which responded to the disaster in Japan in March 2011 under Operation Tomadachi, sued TEPCO for deliberately misrepresenting the radiation risks posed by the disaster.[266] The suit also includes the infant daughter of one of the soldiers as a plaintiff. Their complaint asserts that TEPCO and the government of Japan "acted in concert" to "create an illusionary impression" of safety, while knowing the "extraordinary risks" posed to plaintiffs by actual and known conditions at Daiichi. Furthermore, the complaint asserts that plaintiffs' exposure levels exceeded "the levels of exposure to which those living the same distance from Chernobyl experienced who subsequently developed cancer." Thus, the complaint charges that the likelihood of exposure to cancer has been enhanced and the plaintiffs "face additional and irreparable harm to

DOI: 10.1057/9781137343123

their life expectancy, which has been shortened and cannot be restored to its prior condition." Japan's international liability is uncertain.

Japan announced its interest in joining The Convention on Supplementary Compensation (CSC) for Nuclear Damage, in February 2012.[267] Membership would limit liability to non-Japanese citizens. The CSC offers a uniform and limiting set of compensation standards for victims of nuclear disasters in impacted countries not the origin of the disaster. The convention affords Japan "exclusive jurisdiction" in the event of an accident affecting other countries, while spreading com-pensation costs in excess of 300 million International Monetary Fund special drawing rights among CSC members. The convention also exon-erates manufacturers, placing liability exclusively on operators. The U.S. Deputy Secretary of Energy, Daniel Poneman, promoted Japan's mem-bership in a February 2012 interview with the *Asahi Shimbun*, stating "the events at Fukushima…emphasized the need for a global nuclear liability regime." The convention essentially limits only the liability, but not the incalculable risks, from nuclear accidents.

Ulrich Beck, a sociologist of risk, was interviewed about the Fukushima catastrophe in July 2011. Beck described the Fukushima nuclear event as a "catastrophe" that "is unlimited in space, time and the social dimension. It's the new kind of risk."[268] When asked how such risks are produced, Beck responded: "Risks depend on decision making. The risk depends on the process of modernization. And they're produced with techno-logical innovations and investment." Beck denied that the disaster could have resulted simply from unforeseeable natural catastrophes:

> The decision to build an atomic industry in the area of an earthquake is a political decision; it's not done by nature. It's a political decision, which has to be justified in the public and which has been taken by parliament, by businesses and so on.…I think industries try to define it as something which has been done by nature. But they don't realize that we are living in an age where the decision making is the primary background for these kinds of catastrophes. I think it's very important to realize this because modernity, or even what you could say is the victory of modernity, produces more and more uncontrollable consequences.

Beck observed that with Fukushima and other modern risks stem-ming from human decision making "we have a system of organized irresponsibility: Nobody really is responsible for those consequences. We have a system of organized irresponsibility, and this system has to be changed."[269]

DOI: 10.1057/9781137343123

Military and energy "security" are prioritized by governments over the incalculable human risks posed by nuclear accidents. The "system of organized irresponsibility" requires the populace and the state to assume costs of disasters, even when those costs include health and reproductive harms. Development of national and international settlement protocols for limiting liability for nuclear accidents illustrates how risk is shifted to populations. The next chapter examines the politics of research on the biological effects of radiation. Research studies on effects have been political since the bombing of Japan and widespread atmospheric testing. Research remains political today because of nuclear power plant liability, among other reasons. The discussion will demonstrate that advances in genetic analysis have revealed not only the most subtle, but also potentially deadly, effects of radiation on human DNA. Yet, new understandings are not adequately incorporated into the risk calculus of the ICRP. Consequently, human populations may face health and reproductive risks as a result of the prioritization of the nuclear project over the incalculability of its externalities.

Notes

1   It is worth noting that although this report was produced on 26 October 2010, the file properties indicate the document was modified on 13 March 2011. *Integrity Inspection of Dry Storage Casks and Spent Fuels at Fukushima Daiichi Nuclear Power Station* (16 November 2010), http://www.nirs.org/reactorwatch/accidents/6-1_powerpoint.pdf, date accessed 7 June 2011.
2   *Integrity Inspection of Dry Storage Cask.*
3   J. McCurry (8 June 2011) "Fukushima Nuclear Plant May Have Suffered "Melt-Through": Japan Admits," *The Guardian*, http://www.guardian.co.uk/world/2011/jun/08/fukushima-nuclear-plant-melt-through?CMP=twt_gu, date accessed 8 June 2011.
4   Republic Broadcasting Capital Forum (30 June 2012), http://www.republicbroadcasting.org/podcasts.active.php?programID=74, date accessed 30 June 2012.
5   McCurry "Fukushima Nuclear Plant May Have Suffered." See ""Melt-through" at Fukushima? /Govt report to IAEA Suggests Situation Worse Than Meltdown" (8 June 2011), *The Daily Yomiuri Online*, http://www.yomiuri.co.jp/dy/national/T110607005367.htm, date accessed 8 June 2011. Finally, see J. Ryall (9 June 2011) "Nuclear Fuel Has Melted through Base of Fukushima

DOI: 10.1057/9781137343123

Plant," *The Telegraph*, http://www.telegraph.co.uk/news/8565020/Nuclear-fuel-has-melted-through-base-of-Fukushima-plant.html, date accessed 9 June 2011.

6   Fukushima 311 Watchdogs (2011) "MOX Fuel-Corium-Plutonium in Fukushima Daiichi," http://www.fukushima311watchdogs.org/biblio/9/Mox%20fuel-corium-plutonium%20in%20Fukushima%20Daiichi.pdf, date accessed 8 November 2011. For confirmation of MOX fuel in reactor 3 at the time of the accident see also R. Yoshioka and K. Lino (19 August 2011) "Technical Report: Fukushima Accident Summary," *Association for the Study of Failure*, p. 10, http://www.shippai.org/images/html/news559/FukuAccSummary110819Final.pdf, date accessed 10 October 2011. See also J. Matson (25 March 2011) "MOX Battle: Mixed Oxide Nuclear Fuel Raises Safety Questions," *Scientific American*, http://www.scientificamerican.com/article.cfm?id=mox-fuel-nuclear, date accessed 18 May 2013.

7   Fukushima 311 Watchdogs "MOX."

8   L. Gunter (2011) "Russian Chernobyl Expert Warns of Dire Consequences for Health around Fukushima," *CommonDreams*, http://www.commondreams.org/newswire/2011/03/25-4, date accessed 4 December 2011.

9   Institute of Nuclear Power Operations (November 2011), *Special Report on the Nuclear Accident at the Fukushima Daiichi Nuclear Power Station*, http://www.nei.org/resourcesandstats/documentlibrary/safetyandsecurity/reports/special-report-on-the-nuclear-accident-at-the-fukushima-daiichi-nuclear-power-station, date accessed 1 December 2013.

10   Institute of Nuclear Power Operations, *Special Report*, p. 3.

11   D. McNeil and J. Adelstein (17 August 2011) "The Explosive Truth behind Fukushima's Meltdown," *The Independent*, http://www.independent.co.uk/news/world/asia/the-explosive-truth-behind-fukushimas-meltdown-2338819.html, date accessed 19 August 2011.

12   Blogger Ex-SKF translated and reported the story published in *The Asahi Shimbun* at his blog site. Ex-SKF (23 September 2012), "Now They Tell Us: 1,590 Microsieverts/Hr in Futaba-machi, #Fukushima on March 12, 2011, Before Reactor 1 Explosion, and Vent, Not Explosion, May Have Caused High Radiation," http://ex-skf.blogspot.com/2012/09/now-they-tell-us-1590-microsievertshr.html, date accessed 23 September 2012.

13   Y. Hayashi and A. Morse (16 March 2011) "Setback in Reactor Fight," *The Wall Street Journal*, A1.

14   Y. Hayashi (15 March 2011) "Nuclear Risk Rising in Japan," *The Wall Street Journal*, A1, A12.

15   Hayashi, "Nuclear Risk Rising in Japan," p. A1.

16   Hayashi and Morse "Setback in Reactor Fight," p. A1.

17   T. H. Maugh and R. Vartabedian (11 March 2011) "Damage at Two Japan Nuclear Plants Prompts Evacuations," *The Los Angeles Times*, http://articles.

latimes.com/2011/mar/11/science/la-sci-japan-quake-nuclear-20110312, date accessed 11 March 2011.

18 Cited in McNeil and Adelstein "The Explosive Truth behind Fukushima's Meltdown."

19 Y. Hayashi and R. Smith (12–13 March 2011) "Radiation Leaks at Damaged Plant," *The Wall Street Journal*, A6.

20 The report of a partial meltdown of unit 1 can be found here: K. Hall and C. Williams (15 March 2011) "Fire Erupts Again at Fukushima Daiichi's No. 4 Reactor: Nuclear Fuel Rods Damaged at Other Reactors," *The Los Angeles Times* (15 March 2011), http://articles.latimes.com/2011/mar/15/world/la-fgw-japan-quake-reactor-fire-20110316, date accessed 15 March 2011. The report of criticalities in unit 1 in April here: J. Makinen and T. Maugh (1 April 2011) "Radioactivity Surges Again at Japan Nuclear Plant," *Los Angeles Times*, http://articles.latimes.com/2011/apr/01/science/la-sci-japan-reactor-damage-20110331, date accessed 5 April 2011.

21 A. Morse and M. Obe (29 March 2011), "At Plant, Toxic Pools Threaten to Spill," *The Wall Street Journal*, A12.

22 Hayashi and Morse "Setback in Reactor Fight."

23 "TEPCO's Post-Mortem Shows No. 2 Reactor Main Source of Radiation" (25 May 2012), *The Asahi Shimbun*, http://ajw.asahi.com/article/0311disaster/fukushima/AJ201205250053, date accessed 25 May 2012.

24 Hall and Williams "Fire Erupts Again at Fukushima Daiichi's No. 4 Reactor."

25 Dissensus Japan (14 June 2012) "Local Official: Visible Hot Mass Floated in Air and Fell for Hours after Reactor 3 Exploded – 'Top Secret Images' of Black Smoke Falling – 14 June 2012 post by Minamisoma city council member Koichi Oyama," translated by *Dissensus Japan,* http://mak55.exblog.jp/16050533/, date accessed 30 June 2012.

26 See for discussion W. Broad and H. Tabuchi (14 March 2011) "In Stricken Fuel-Cooling Pools, a Danger for the Longer Term," *The Wall Street Journal*, 14 March 2011, http://www.nytimes.com/2011/03/15/world/asia/15fuel.html?_r=2, date accessed 14 March 2011.

27 R. Alvarez, J. Beyea, K. Janberg, J. Kang, E. Lyman, A. Macfarlane, G. Thompson, and F. von Hippel (2003) "Reducing the Hazards from Stored Spent Power-Reactor Fuel in the United States," *Science and Global Security*, 11.1, 1–51.

28 S. Goldenberg (16 March 2011) "Japan Nuclear Crisis: Fire in Fuel Pools 'Would Raise Radiation Exposure'," *The Guardian*, http://www.guardian.co.uk/environment/2011/mar/16/japan-nuclear-fire-fuel-pools-radiation, date accessed 16 March 2011.

29 Broad and Tabuchi, "In Stricken Fuel-Cooling Pools."

30 See image at http://www.bt.dk/sites/default/files-dk/node-images/927/3/3927084-japan-nuclearradiation.jpg, date accessed 7 August 2013.

DOI: 10.1057/9781137343123

31   R. Smith and G. Naik (17 March 2011) "Spent Fuel Rods Pose Big Risk," *The Wall Street Journal*, A12 and Goldenberg, "Japan Nuclear Crisis."

32   A. Gundersen (26 April 2011) "Gundersen Postulates Unit 3 Explosion May Have Been Prompt Criticality in Fuel Pool," *Fairewinds*, http://fairewinds. com/content/gundersen-postulates-unit-3-explosion-may-have-been-prompt-criticality-fuel-pool, date accessed 26 April 2011.

33   Hayashi and Morse "Setback in Reactor Fight."

34   Smith and Naik "Spent Fuel Rods Pose Big Risk."

35   Maugh and Vartabedian, "Damage at Two Japan Nuclear Plants Prompts Evacuations."

36   The press release has since been removed from the IAEA webpage. It was originally found at http://www.iaea.org/press/?p=1248, date accessed 30 March 2011.

37   http://www.iaea.org/press/?p=1252, date accessed 30 march 2011.

38   Hall and Williams, "Fire Erupts Again at Fukushima Daiichi's No. 4 Reactor."

39   Goldenberg "Japan Nuclear Crisis."

40   T. Maugh (19 March 2011) "Electric Power Partially Restored at Japan Nuclear Plant," *The Los Angeles Times*, http://articles.latimes.com/2011/mar/19/science/la-sci-japan-reactor-damage-20110319, date accessed 20 March 2011.

41   "TEPCO Injects" (20 June 2011), *NHK*, http://www3.nhk.or.jp/daily/english/20_03.html, date accessed 20 June 2011.

42   H. Hattori and K. Takeuchi (29 June 2012) "AEC Chairman: Major Change Needed in Reprocessing Nuclear Fuel," *The Asahi Shimbun*, http://ajw.asahi.com/article/0311disaster/fukushima/AJ201206290123, date accessed 30 June 2012.

43   K. Nagata (9 March 2013) "Water is Both the Savior and the Bane at Fukushima No. 1," *The Japan Times*, http://www.japantimes.co.jp/news/2013/03/09/national/water-is-both-the-savior-and-the-bane-at-fukushima-no-1/#.UTof11eQPnd, date accessed 10 March 2013.

44   U.S. Nuclear Regulatory Commission (16 March 2011) "Official Transcript of Proceedings of Japan's Fukushima Daiichi ET Audio File," p. 62, http://pbadupws.nrc.gov/docs/ML1205/ML12052A108.pdf, date accessed 7 May 2011.

45   U.S. NRC, "Official Transcript," March 16.

46   H. Tabuchi and A. Pollack (7 April 2011) "Japan Is Struck by Powerful Aftershock," *The New York Times*, http://www.nytimes.com/2011/04/08/world/asia/08japan.html?_r=1&, date accessed 8 April 2011.

47   J. Glanz and W. Broad (5 April 2011) "U.S. Sees Array of New Threats at Japan's Nuclear Plant," *The New York Times*, http://www.nytimes.com/2011/04/06/world/asia/06nuclear.html?pagewanted=all&_r=0, date accessed 6 April 2011.

48   R. Alvarez (May 2011) *Spent Nuclear Fuel Pools in the U.S.: Reducing the Deadly Risks of Storage* (Institute of Policy Studies), pp. 5–7, http://www.ips-dc.org/files/3200/spent_nuclear_fuel_pools_in_the_us.pdf, date accessed 19 June 2011

DOI: 10.1057/9781137343123

49 "Plutonium Found in Soil at Okuma" (7 June 2011), *The Japan Times*, http://www.japantimes.co.jp/text/nn20110607a4.html, date accessed 7 June 2011.

50 "Plutonium Traces Detected at 10 Locations in Fukushima" (23 August 2012), *The Japan Times*, http://www.japantimes.co.jp/text/nn20120823a4.html, date accessed 23 August 2012.

51 T. Inajima and Y. Okada (2 November 2011) "TEPCO Detects Nuclear Fission at Damaged Fukushima Power Station," *Business Week*, http://www.businessweek.com/news/2011-11-02/TEPCO-detects-nuclear-fission-at-fukushima-station.html, date accessed 2 November 2011.

52 F. Dalnoki-Veress (28 March 2011) "What Was the Cause of the High C1–38 Radioactivity in the Fukushima Daiichi Reactor #1," http://lewis.armscontrolwonk.com/files/2011/03/Cause_of_the_high_Cl38_Radioactivity.pdf, date accessed 30 March 2011.

53 I have been watching the two Fukushima webcams and have screen shots of events. The TEPCO webcam is available at http://www.TEPCO.co.jp/nu/f1-np/camera/index-j.html and the TBS webcam at http://www.youtube.com/user/tbsnewsi/featured, date accessed June 2011 to present.

54 K. Ohmae (28 October 2011) "Lessons of Fukushima Dai-ichi," available at http://pr.bbt757.com/eng/. Full report at http://pr.bbt757.com/eng/pdf/finalrepo_111225.pdf, date accessed 30 October 2011.

55 Cited in Maugh and Vartabedian, "Damage at Two Japan Nuclear Plants Prompts Evacuations."

56 Tabuchi and Pollack, "Japan Is Struck by Powerful Aftershock."

57 Ex-SKF (3 July 2011) " 'Now They Tell Us' Series: Depleted Uranium Storage Facility Next to Cosmo Oil Refinery in Chiba Burned after Earthquake Hit on March 11," http://ex-skf.blogspot.com/2011/07/now-they-tell-us-series-depleted.html, date accessed 3 July 2011.

58 "TEPCO Post-Mortem Shows No. 2 Reactor Main Source of Radiation" (25 May 2012), *The Asahi Shimbun*, http://ajw.asahi.com/article/0311disaster/fukushima/AJ201205250053, date accessed 25 May 2012.

59 W. Zhang, J. Friese, and K. Ungar (2013) "The Ambient Gamma Dose-Rate and the Inventory of Fission Products Estimations with the Soil Samples Collected at Canadian Embassy in Tokyo during Fukushima Nuclear Accident," *Journal of Radio analytical and Nuclear Chemistry*, 296.1, 69–73.

60 J. Zheng, K. Tagami, Y. Watanabe, S. Uchida, T. Aono, N. Ishii, S. Yoshida, Y. Kubota, S. Fuma, and S. Ihara (8 March 2012) "Isotopic Evidence of Plutonium Release into the Environment from the Fukushima DNPP Accident," *Scientific Reports*, 2, http://www.nature.com/srep/2012/120308/srep00304/full/srep00304.html, date accessed 9 March 2012.

61 N. Kaneyasu, H. Ohashi, F. Suzuki, T. Okuda, and F. Ikemori (2012) "Sulfate Aerosol as a Potential Transport Medium of Radiocesium from the

DOI: 10.1057/9781137343123

Fukushima Nuclear Accident," *Environmental Science and Technology*, 46.11, 5720–5726.

62   C. Armstrong, M. Nyman, T. Shvareva, G. Sigmon, P. Burns, and A. Navrotsky (2012) "Uranyl Peroxide Enhanced Nuclear Fuel Corrosion in Seawater," *Proceedings of the National Academy of Sciences*, 109.6, 1874–1877.

63   A. Priyadarshi, G. Dominguez, and M. Thiemens (2011) "Evidence of Neutron Leakage at the Fukushima Nuclear Plant from Measurements of Radioactive ^{35}S in California," *Proceedings of the National Academy of Sciences*, 108.35, 14422–14425.

64   G. Wetherbee, T. Debey, M. Nilles, C. Lehmann, and D. Gay. (2012) "Fission Products in National Atmospheric Deposition Program-West Deposition Samples Prior to and Following the Fukushima Dai-ichi Nuclear Power Plant Incident, March 8–April 5, 2011," U.S. Geological Survey Open-File Report 2011, 1277, p. 6.

65   Taped video discussion with Prof. Robert Jacobs on social mobilization in Japan after Fukushima published by Jagar Uttarakhand: "Professor in Japan Blasts Gov't, TEPCO: 'These are Lies, They're Absolutely Lies' " (9 July 2012), *Enenews*, http://enenews.com/professor-japan-blasts-govt-TEPCO-lies-theyre-absolutely-lies-video, date accessed 9 July 2012.

66   The Fukushima Nuclear Accident Independent Investigation Commission, Japan National Diet (2012) "The Official Report of the Fukushima Nuclear Accident Independent Investigation Commission (2012)," Executive Summary, available at http://naiic.go.jp/wp-content/uploads/2012/07/NAIIC_report_hi_res2.pdf, date accessed 7 February 2012

67   "TEPCO Seeks More Govt Support as Fukushima Costs Soar" (7 November 2012), *The Asahi Shimbun*, http://ajw.asahi.com/article/0311disaster/fukushima/AJ201211070086, date accessed 7 November 2012.

68   The Fukushima Nuclear Accident Independent Investigation Commission, pp. 18–19.

69   "Timeline: Japan Power Plant Crisis" (13 March 2011), *BBC News*, http://www.bbc.co.uk/news/science-environment-12722719, date accessed 29 October 2012.

70   Institute of Nuclear Power Operations (November 2011) "Special Report on the Nuclear Accident at the Fukushima Daiichi Nuclear Power Station," http://www.nei.org/resourcesandstats/documentlibrary/safetyandsecurity/reports/special-report-on-the-nuclear-accident-at-the-fukushima-daiichi-nuclear-power-station, date accessed 7 July 2012.

71   The Fukushima Nuclear Accident Independent Investigation Commission, p. 19.

72   H. Sunaoshi and K. Kanai (18 June 2012) "Government Ignored U.S. Radiation Monitoring Data in Days after 3/11," *The Asahi Shimbun*, http://ajw.asahi.com/article/0311disaster/fukushima/AJ201206180048, date accessed 19 June 2012.

DOI: 10.1057/9781137343123

73 D. McNeill (15 June 2011) "Who's Telling the Truth on the Fukushima Meltdown?" *CNNGo.Com*, http://www.cnngo.com/tokyo/life/tell-me-about-it/david-mcneill-whos-telling-truth-fukushima-448215#ixzz1PMTJwTk1, date accessed 19 July 2011.

74 "Timeline: Japan Power Plant Crisis."

75 "Ex-Regulator Resigns from TEPCO," (19 April 2011), *Reuters* (video), http://www.reuters.com/article/video/idUSTRE73I10E20110419?videoId=204721879, date accessed 19 April 2011.

76 L. King, R. Vartabedian and T. Maugh (15 March 2011) "Japan Fears a Nuclear Disaster after Reactor Breach," *The Los Angeles Times*, http://articles.latimes.com/2011/mar/15/world/la-fg-japan-quake-20110315, date accessed 15 March 2011.

77 Andrew Morse and Mitsuru Obe (26–27 March 2011) "Setback for Japan at Rogue Reactors," *The Wall Street Journal*, A1.

78 N. Shirouzu and R. Smith (17 March 2011) "U.S. Sounds Alarm on Radiation," *The Wall Street Journal*, A1.

79 Y. Koh, D. Wakabayashi, and M. Inada (4 April 2011) "Worries Mount over Residents Still near Plant," *The Wall Street Journal*, A11.

80 F. Atsushi (12 September 2011) "Understanding the Ongoing Nuclear Disaster in Fukushima: A 'Two-Headed Dragon' Descends into the Earth's Biosphere," translated by M. Bourdaghs, *Asia-Pacific Journal*, 9.37, http://www.japanfocus.org/-Fujioka-Atsushi/3599, date accessed 12 September 2011.

81 H. Tabuchi, K. Bradsher, and A. Pollack (13 April 2011) "Japanese Officials on Defensive as Nuclear Alert Level Rises," *The New York Times*, http://www.nytimes.com/2011/04/13/world/asia/13japan.html, date accessed 14 April 2011.

82 Tabuchi, Bradsher, and Pollack "Japanese Officials on Defensive."

83 "Nuclear Accident Disclosure" (8 July 2011), *Japan Times*, http://search.japantimes.co.jp/cgi-bin/ed20110708a1.html, date accessed 10 July 2011.

84 "Japan Ignored Own Radiation Forecasts from Very Beginning" (10 August 2011), *Japan Today*, http://www.japantoday.com/category/national/view/japan-ignored-own-radiation-forecasts-from-very-beginning, date accessed 12 August 2011.

85 "Government Knew Radiation Fallout Forecast Reliable" (11 June 2012), *NHK*, http://www3.nhk.or.jp/daily/english/20120611_32.html, date accessed 11 June 2011.

86 Y. Hayashi (29 September 2011) "Japan Officials Failed to Hand out Radiation Pills in Quake's Aftermath," *The Wall Street Journal*, http://online.wsj.com/article/SB10001424052970204010604576596321581004368.html, date accessed 30 September 2011.

87 Sunaoshi and Kanai "Government Ignored U.S. Radiation."

88 Sunaoshi and Kanai "Government Ignored U.S. Radiation."

89 Sunaoshi and Kanai "Government Ignored U.S. Radiation."

DOI: 10.1057/9781137343123

90   "Japan Admits 3 Nuclear Meltdowns, More Radiation Leaked into Sea"
     (3 June 2011), *Democracy Now*, http://www.democracynow.org/2011/6/10/
     as_japan_nuclear_crisis_worsens_citizen, date accessed 29 June 2011.

91   "45% of Kids in Fukushima Survey Had Thyroid Exposure to Radiation"
     (5 July 2011), *The Mainichi*, http://mdn.mainichi.jp/mdnnews/
     news/20110705p2g00m0dm079000c.html, date accessed 6 July 2011.

92   "Up to 1/7 of Fukushima May Be Contaminated" (15 September
     2011), *The Mainichi*, http://mdn.mainichi.jp/mdnnews/
     news/20110915p2g00m0dm114000c.html, date accessed 16 September 2011.

93   Atsushi "Understanding the Ongoing Nuclear disaster in Fukushima."

94   S. Sekine (25 May 2013) "Strict Radiation Reference Levels Shunned
     to Stem Fukushima Exodus," *The Asahi Shimbun*, http://ajw.asahi.com/
     article/0311disaster/fukushima/AJ201305250053, date accessed 26 May 2013.

95   A. Takada (24 July 2011) "Japan's Food-Chain Threat Multiplies as
     Fukushima Radiation Spreads," *Bloomberg*, http://www.bloomberg.com/
     news/2011-07-24/threat-to-japanese-food-chain-multiplies-as-cesium-
     contamination-spreads.html, date accessed 24 July 2011.

96   "Testing System Urgently Needed after Discovery of Radiation-Tainted
     Beef" (13 July 2011), *The Mainichi*, http://mdn.mainichi.jp/perspectives/
     news/20110713p2a00m0na001000c.html, date accessed 13 July 2011.

97   "Colossal blunder on Radioactive Cattle Feed" (2011, July 18), *The Yomiuri
     Shimbun* http://www.yomiuri.co.jp/dy/national/T110717002520.htm, date
     accessed 19 July 2011.

98   Atsushi "Understanding the Ongoing Nuclear Disaster in Fukushima."

99   Y-G Zhu and E. Smolders (2000) "Plant Uptake of Radiocaesium: A Review
     of Mechanisms, Regulation and Application," *Journal of Experimental Botany*,
     51.351, 1635–1645.

100 Ministry of Education, Culture, Sports, Science and Technology
     (2012) "Readings of Radioactivity Level in Drinking Water by
     Prefecture April–June, 2012, http://radioactivity.mext.go.jp/ja/
     contents/6000/5879/24/194m_0801.pdf, date accessed 19 November 2012.

101 "Rubble from Quake- and Tsunami-Hit Areas to Be Disposed in Tokyo"
     (29 September 2011), *The Mainichi*, http://mainichi.jp/english/english/
     mdnnews/news/20110929p2a00m0na010000c.html, date accessed 30
     September 2011.

102 "Radioactive Ash Causes Kashiwa Incinerators to Shut Down" (4 November
     2011), *Japan Today*, http://www.japantoday.com/category/national/view/
     radioactive-ash-causes-shutdown-of-kashiwa-incinerators, date accessed 5
     November 2011.

103 "Storage Space to Be Built at 2 Sites in Fukushima for Tsunami Debris" (8
     April 2012), *The Mainichi*, http://mainichi.jp/english/english/newsselect/
     news/20120408p2g00m0dm055000c.html, date accessed 9 April 2012.

DOI: 10.1057/9781137343123

104 "Decontamination Work Begins in Fukushima Prefecture City Amid
     Concerns over Incinerator Plans" (27 July 2012), *The Mainichi*, http://
     mainichi.jp/english/english/newsselect/news/20120727p2a00m0na010000c.
     html, date accessed 29 July 2012.

105 A. Zolbert (8 November 2012) "Japan Earthquake and Tsunami Recovery
     Still Underway" *KSDK News*, http://www.ksdk.com/news/article/346639/28/
     Japan-earthquake-and-tsunami-recovery-still-underway, date accessed 9
     November 2012.

106 Institute for Energy and Environmental (May 2012) "Incineration of
     Radioactive and Mixed Waste," http://ieer.org/resource/factsheets/
     incineration-radioactive-mixed/, date accessed 9 November 2012.

107 Y. Iwahana, A. Ohbuchi, Y. Koike, M. Kitano, and T. Nakamura (2013)
     "Radioactive Nuclides in the Incinerator Ashes of Municipal Solid Waste before
     and after the Fukushima Nuclear Power Plant," *Annals of Science*, 29.1, 61–66.

108 S. Tokonami, M. Hosoda, S. Akiba, A. Sorimachi, I. Kashiwakura,
     and M. Balonov (12 July 2012), "Thyroid Doses for Evacuees from the
     Fukushima Nuclear Accident," *Scientific Reports*, http://www.nature.com/
     srep/2012/120712/srep00507/pdf/srep00507.pdf, date accessed 13 July 2012

109 "Thyroid Screenings Detect Relatively High Exposure" (9 March 2012),
     NHK, http://www3.nhk.or.jp/daily/english/20120309_18.html, date accessed
     9 March 2012.

110 "Fukushima Residents' Urine Now Radioactive," (27 June 2011), *Japan
     Times*, http://search.japantimes.co.jp/cgi-bin/nn20110627a2.html, date
     accessed 27 June 2011.

111 "Japan Groups Alarmed by Radioactive Soil," (5 June 2011), *Agence
     France-Presse*, http://www.google.com/hostednews/afp/article/
     ALeqM5ivr747xKaxw9RGq5zMSDO-On_WRQ?docId=CNG.62875ee35cc2
     8aa30725ee1bfd4cfbde.111, date accessed 20 June 2011.

112 "Japan Admits 3 Nuclear Meltdowns, More Radiation Leaked into Sea."

113 "Studying the Fukushima Aftermath: 'People Are Suffering from
     Radiophobia'" (19 August 2011), *Der Spiegel*, http://www.spiegel.de/
     international/world/0,1518,780810,00.html, date accessed 4 September 2011.

114 J. Hongo (10 June 2011) "Widen Evacuation Zone for Children, Pregnant
     Women: Greenpeace Chief," *Japan Times*, http://search.japantimes.co.jp/
     cgi-bin/nn20110610a6.html, date accessed 11 June 2011.

115 S. Nomura (14 June 2012) "Radioactive 'Black Soil' Patches," *The Asahi
     Shimbun Weekly Area*, http://ajw.asahi.com/article/0311disaster/fukushima/
     AJ201206140067, date accessed 16 June 2012.

116 "TEPCO Post Mortem."

117 H. Caldicott (September 2011) "Arnold Gundersen with a Fukushima
     update," *If You Love This Planet*, http://ifyoulovethisplanet.org/?p=4952, date
     accessed 30 September 2011.

DOI: 10.1057/9781137343123

118　Ex-SKF (July 2011) "Radiation in Fukushima City," http://ex-skf.blogspot. com/2011/07/radiation-in-fukushima-city-order-of.html, date accessed 31 July 2011.

119　"High Levels of Radioactivity Found Extensively" (20 July 2011), *NHK*, http:// www3.nhk.or.jp/daily/english/21_06.html, date accessed 21 July 2011.

120　"Group: Ministry May Have Manipulated Fukushima Radiation Readings" (6 October 2012), *The Asahi Shimbun*, http://ajw.asahi.com/article/0311disaster/ fukushima/AJ201210060041, date accessed 7 October 2012.

121　Fukushima Diary (7 November 2012) "Japanese Gov Admitted Monitored Radiation Level is Indicated to be 10% Lower Than Actual," http:// fukushima-diary.com/2012/11/japanese-gov-admitted-monitored-radiation- level-is-indicated-to-be-10-lower-than-actual/, date accessed 8 November 2012; and Ex-SKF (7 November 2012) "Japanese Government Now Admits 675 Radiation Monitoring Posts Show '10% Lower' Than Actual Levels, 'Beyond Expectation' Says Ministry of Education," http://ex-skf.blogspot. com/2012/11/japanese-government-now-admits-675.html, date accessed 8 November 2012.

122　Cited in M. Penney (1 July 2011) "Japanese Cancer Expert on the Fukushima Situation," *The Asia Pacific Journal: Japan Focus*, http://japanfocus.org/events/ view/100, date accessed 10 July 2011.

123　See M. Kaku (21 June 2011) "Fukushima Still a Ticking Time Bomb," *CNN in the Arena Blogs*, http://inthearena.blogs.cnn.com/2011/06/21/fukushima- still-a-ticking-time-bomb/, date accessed 25 June 2011.

124　"Nitrogen Injection Could Be Delayed at Fukushima" (6 July 2011), *NHK*, http://www3.nhk.or.jp/daily/english/07_18.html, date accessed 9 July 2011.

125　Based on my personal daily observations 1 April 2011 through present, available at http://www.TEPCO.co.jp/nu/f1-np/camera/index-j.html.

126　Kaku, "Fukushima Still a Ticking Time Bomb."

127　J. McCurry (1 June 2011) "Fukushima Effect: Japan Schools Take Health Precautions in Radiation Zone," *The Guardian*, http://www. guardian.co.uk/world/2011/jun/01/fukushima-effect-japan-schools- radiation?INTCMP=SRCH, date accessed 10 June 2011.

128　For a critical discussion of Japanese children's exposure to radiation see *K. Tatsuhiko (2011) "Radiation Effects on Health: Protect the Children of Fukushima," The Asia-Pacific Journal*, http://japanfocus.org/-Kodama- Tatsuhiko/3587, date accessed 12 January 2012.

129　McCurry, "Fukushima Effect."

130　*Say-Peace Project (20 June 2011) "Protecting Children against Radiation: Japanese Citizens Take Radiation Protection into Their Own Hands," The Asia-Pacific Journal*, http://japanfocus.org/-Say_Peace-Project/3549. *The pamphlet can be viewed* http://www.mhlw.go.jp/stf/houdou/2r98520000014hcd- img/2r98520000014hdu.pdf, date accessed 25 June 2011.

DOI: 10.1057/9781137343123

131 "Ministry Sorry for School Radiation Flipflop" (12 June 2012), *NHK,* http://
www3.nhk.or.jp/daily/english/20120612_13.html, date accessed 14 June 2012.

132 J. Ogura (14 June 2011) "Japan to Hand Out Radiation Meters To Kids Near
Crippled Plant," *CNN,* http://edition.cnn.com/2011/WORLD/asiapcf/06/14/
japan.nuclear.crisis/index.html?eref=edition, date accessed 20 July 2011.

133 Ex-SKF (15 June 2011) "Radiation in Japan: Nosebleed, Diarrhea, Lack of
Energy in Children in Koriyama City, Fukushima," *Ex-SKF,* http://ex-skf.
blogspot.com/2011/06/radiation-in-japan-nosebleed-diarrhea.html, date
accessed 16 June 2011.

134 Tatsuhiko "*Radiation Effects on Health.*"

135 "Radiation Detected in Fukushima Children's Urine" (30 June 2011), *NHK,*
http://www3nhk.or.jp/daily/english/30_35.html, date accessed 30 June 2011.

136 Tatsuhiko "Radiation Effects on Health."

137 "Small Amount of Cesium Detected in Fukushima Children's Urine" (1 July
2012), *Kyodo,* http://english.kyodonews.jp/news/2012/07/166838.html, date
accessed 2 July 2012.

138 W. Tchertkoff (2008) *Nuclear Controversies,* http://www.youtube.com/
watch?v=8qqhm_ZrfhE&feature=relmfu, date accessed 9 August 2011.

139 Y. I. Bandazhevsky (2003) "Chronic Cs-137 Incorporation in Children's
Organs," *Swiss Medical Weekly,* 133, 488–490, http://tchernobyl.verites.free.fr/
sciences/smw-Bandazhevsky_chronicCs137.pdf, date accessed 7 June 2013.

140 *Tatsuhiko (2011) "Radiation Effects on Health,"* http://japanfocus.org/-Kodama-
Tatsuhiko/3587, date accessed 12 January 2012.

141 Y. Oiwa (11 July 2012) "Study Finds Lifetime Thyroid Doses of Radiation
in Fukushima Children," *The Asahi Shimbun,* http://ajw.asahi.com/
article/0311disaster/fukushima/AJ201207110058, date accessed 12 July 2012.

142 Y. Oiwa (14 February 2013) Questions Raised over Testing Methods for
Thyroid Gland Doses in Fukushima, *The Asahi Shimbun,* http://ajw.asahi.
com/article/0311disaster/fukushima/AJ201302140072, date accessed 14
February 2013.

143 "Nuclear Commission Erases Children's Exposure Data" (11 August 2011),
NHK, http://www3.nhk.or.jp/daily/english/11_14.html, date accessed 12
August 2011.

144 Sources: Actual research document available at http://www.pref.fukushima.
jp/imu/kenkoukanri/240426shiryou.pdf, date accessed 30 April 2012. The
Peace Philosophy department posted the results at http://peacephilosophy.
blogspot.com/2012/04/blog-post_28.html, date accessed 30 April 2012
Translation provided by Fukushima Diary: http://fukushima-diary.
com/2012/04/thyroid-nodules-rate-in-fukushima-is-20-time-higher-than-in-
chernobyl/?utm_source=feedburner&utm_medium=feed&utm_campaign=F
eed%3A+FukushimaDiary+%28Fukushima+Diary%29, date accessed
30 April 2012.

DOI: 10.1057/9781137343123

145   J. Ryall (19 July 2012) "Nearly 36pc of Fukushima Children Diagnosed with Abnormal Thyroid Growths," *The Telegraph*, http://www.telegraph.co.uk/news/worldnews/asia/japan/9410702/Nearly-36pc-of-Fukushima-children-diagnosed-with-abnormal-thyroid-growths.html, date accessed 20 July 2012.

146   A. Haworth (22 February 2013) "After Fukushima: Families on Edge of Meltdown," *The Guardian*, http://www.guardian.co.uk/environment/2013/feb/24/divorce-after-fukushima-nuclear-disaster, date accessed 24 February 2013.

147   C. Busby (24 June 2011) "Statement of Chris Busby in Relation to Provisional Injunction Against Education Committee of Koryama City, Fukushima to Evacuate the Children for the Radioactively Contaminated Area Being filed on 24th June 2011," http://1am.sakura.ne.jp/Nuclear/110623Statement-BusbyE.pdf, date accessed 30 June 2011.

148   The film is not yet publicly available, but a trailer can be found at "A2" (2012), http://www.a2documentary.com/. More information can be found at *Documenting Ian Blog* http://ianthomasash.blogspot.jp/, date accessed 11 November 2012.

149   I. T. Ash (5 November 2012) "The Mothers and Their Children," *Documenting Ian Blog*, http://ianthomasash.blogspot.jp/2012/11/the-mothers-and-their-children-part-2.html, date accessed 19 November 2012.

150   S. Zeltzer (11 November 2012) "One Day in Fukushima," *Counterpunch*, http://www.counterpunch.org/2012/11/09/one-day-in-fukushima/, date accessed 12 November 2012.

151   A. Koerblein (10 January 2013) "Infant Mortality in Japan after Fukushima," *Strahlentelex mit Elektrosmog Report*, http://www.strahlentelex.de/Infant_mortality_in_Japan_after_Fukushima.pdf, date accessed 11 February 2013.

152   A. Körblein and H. Küchenhoff (1997) "Perinatal Mortality in Germany Following the Chernobyl Accident," *Radiation and Environmental Biophysics*, 36.1, 3–7, http://www.alfred-koerblein.de/chernobyl/downloads/KoKu1997.pdf, date accessed 7 August 2011.

153   Associated Press (25 April 2013) "Japan Court Rejects Demand to Evacuate Fukushima Children," *The Asahi Shimbun*, http://ajw.asahi.com/article/0311disaster/fukushima/AJ201304250125, date accessed 20 May 2013.

154   Associated Press (15 April 2013) "Lawsuit Seeks Evacuation of Fukushima Children," *The Asahi Shimbun,* http://ajw.asahi.com/article/0311disaster/fukushima/AJ201304150003, date accessed 20 May 2013.

155   P. Dvorak (14 June 2011) "Japanese Nuclear Cleanup Workers Detail Lax Safety Practices at Plant," *The Wall Street Journal*, A1, A12.

156   Y. Oiwa (1 December 2012) "High Thyroid Radiation Doses in 178 Fukushima Workers," *The Asahi Shimbun*, http://ajw.asahi.com/

DOI: 10.1057/9781137343123

article/0311disaster/life_and_death/AJ201212010050, date accessed 7 December 2012.

157   I. Perlingieri (4 May 2011) "No Protection for Fukushima's 'Expendable' Citizens or Us," *Jeff Rense*, http://www.rense.com/general94/noprot.htm, date accessed 9 July 2011.

158   "Whereabouts of 30 Nuclear Power Plant Subcontractors Unknown: Health Ministry" (21 June 2011), *The Mainichi*, http://mdn.mainichi.jp/mdnnews/news/20110621p2a00m0na005000c.html, date accessed 22 June 2011.

159   "TEPCO Says It Has Lost Contact with 143 Nuclear Plant Workers" (10 August 2011), *Japan Today*, http://www.japantoday.com/category/national/view/TEPCO-says-it-has-lost-contact-with-143-nuclear-plant-workers, date accessed 11 August 2011.

160   O. Mitsuru (31 August 2012) "Japan Finds Radiation Spread over a Wide Area," *The Wall Street Journal*, A11.

161   Reuters (21 July 2012) "Japan Probes Under-Reporting of Fukushima Radiation Dosage," *The Washington Post*, http://www.washingtonpost.com/world/japan-probes-under-reporting-of-fukushima-radiation-dosage/2012/07/21/gJQAdgJwoW_story.html?wpisrc=nl_headlines, date accessed 22 July 2012.

162   M. Aoki (5 November 2012) "Special Allowance Not Reaching Workers Involved in Disaster Cleanup," *The Asahi Shimbun*, http://ajw.asahi.com/article/0311disaster/fukushima/AJ201211050079, date accessed 6 November 2012.

163   M. Aoki and T. Tada (9 December 2012) "Worker Wants New Government to Secure Safety at Fukushima Plant," *The Asahi Shimbun*, http://ajw.asahi.com/article/0311disaster/fukushima/AJ201212090052, date accessed 10 December 2012.

164   M. Aoki (21 November 2012) "Most Fukushima Nuke Plant Workers Ineligible for Free Cancer Checks," *The Asahi Shimbun*, http://ajw.asahi.com/article/0311disaster/fukushima/AJ201211220056, date accessed 22 November 2012.

165   Cited in H. Tabuchi (25 June 2012) "Fears Accompany Fishermen in Japanese Disaster Region," *The New York Times*, http://www.nytimes.com/2012/06/26/world/asia/fears-accompany-fishermen-in-japanese-disaster-region.html?nl=todaysheadlines&emc=edit_th_20120626, date accessed 26 June 2012.

166   "Fukushima Nuclear Pollution in Sea was World's Worst: French Institute" (28 October 2011), *Japan Today*, http://www.japantoday.com/category/national/view/fukushima-nuclear-pollution-in-sea-was-worlds-worst-french-institute, date accessed 29 October 2011.

167   N. Casacuberta, P. Masque, J. Garcia-Orellana, R. Garcia-Tenorio, and K. Buesseler (2013) "90Sr and 89Sr in Seawater off Japan as a Consequence

DOI: 10.1057/9781137343123

of the Fukushima Dai-ichi Nuclear Accident," *Biogeosciences Discussion*, 10, 2039–2067, p. 2047.

168   "Fukushima Disaster Produces World's Worst Nuclear Sea Pollution" (28 October 2011), *The Maritime Executive*, http://www.maritime-executive.com/ article/fukushima-disaster-produces-world-s-worst-nuclear-sea-pollution, date accessed 29 October 2011.

169   "New N-Crisis Video Made Available" (2 December 2012), *Jiji Press*, http:// www.yomiuri.co.jp/dy/national/T121201003241.htm, date accessed 4 December 2012.

170   T. Sugimoto and H. Kimura (1 December 2012) "TEPCO Failed to Respond to Dire Warning of Radioactive Water Leaks at Fukushima," *The Asahi Shimbun*, http://ajw.asahi.com/article/0311disaster/fukushima/ AJ201212010037, date accessed 2 December 2012.

171   R. Yoshida (21 May 2013) "Fukushima No. 1 Can't Keep Its Head above Tainted Water," *Japan Times*, http://www.japantimes.co.jp/news/2013/05/21/ reference/fukushima-no-1-cant-keep-its-head-above-tainted-water/#. UZpke8oQNX9, date accessed 21 May 2013.

172   R. Mackey and R. Somaiya (1 November 2011) "Japanese Official Drinks Water From Fukushima Reactor Buildings," *The New York Times,* http:// thelede.blogs.nytimes.com/2011/11/01/japanese-official-drinks-water-from-fukushima-reactor-buildings/, date accessed 3 November 2011.

173   "TEPCO Reports Drop in Water Injection Rate at N-plant" (1 September 2012), *Yomiuri*, http://www.yomiuri.co.jp/dy/national/T120831004812.htm, date accessed 2 September 2012.

174   Kimura, S. (8 April 2013) "Defect Could Affect All Radioactive Water Storage Tanks at Fukushima Plant," *The Asahi Shimbun*, http://ajw.asahi. com/article/0311disaster/fukushima/AJ201304080089, date accessed 9 April 2013.

175   "Japan Struggling to Store Radioactive Water" (25 October 2012), *Al Jazeera*, http://www.aljazeera.com/news/asia-pacific/2012/10/2012102510561941251. html, date accessed 26 October 2012. See also M. Yamaguchi (25 October 2012) "AP Interview: Japan Nuke Plant Water Worries Rise," *Yahoo*, http:// news.yahoo.com/ap-interview-japan-nuke-plant-water-worries-rise-064339732.html, date accessed 26 October 2012.

176   World Nuclear Association "Fukushima Accident."

177   "TEPCO to Dump Groundwater to Ease Crisis at Fukushima Nuclear Plant."

178   Kimura "Defect Could Affect All Radioactive Water Storage Tanks at Fukushima Plant."

179   "TEPCO to Dump Groundwater to Ease Crisis at Fukushima Nuclear Plant" (8 May 2013), http://ajw.asahi.com/article/0311disaster/fukushima/ AJ201305080062, date accessed 9 May 2013.

DOI: 10.1057/9781137343123

180   Yoshida "Fukushima No. 1 Can't Keep its Head Above Tainted Water."
181   S. Kimura (6 April 2013) "120 Tons of Contaminated Water Leaks at Fukushima Nuclear Plant," *The Asahi Shimbun*, http://ajw.asahi.com/article/0311disaster/fukushima/AJ201304060038, date accessed 7 April 2013.
182   Yoshida "Fukushima No. 1 Can't Keep its Head Above Tainted Water."
183   Mackey and Somaiya "Japanese Official Drinks."
184   K. Buesseler, M. Aoyama, and M. Fukasawa (2011) "Impacts of the Fukushima Nuclear Power Plants on Marine Radioactivity," *Environmental Science and Technology*, 45.23, 9931–9935.
185   A. Roslin (19 October 2011) "What Are Officials Hiding about Fukushima?" *Straight.com*, http://www.straight.com/article-491941/vancouver/what-are-officials-hiding-about-fukushima?page=0%2C2, date accessed 20 October 2011.
186   K. Buesseler (26 October 2012) "Fishing for Answers off Fukushima," *Science Magazine*, 338, 480–482.
187   TEPCO (21 September 2012) "Nuclides Analysis Result of the Radioactive Materials in the Seawater Coast, Fukushima Daiichi Nuclear Power Station," http://www.TEPCO.co.jp/en/nu/fukushima-np/f1/images/2012sampling/seawater_120921-e.pdf, date accessed 9 October 2012.
188   "Cesium Levels in Fish off Fukushima Not dropping" (26 October 2012), *The Asahi Shimbun*, http://ajw.asahi.com/article/0311disaster/fukushima/AJ201210260047, date accessed 27 October 2012.
189   "25,800 Becquerels of Cesium Detected in Fish Caught Off Fukushima" (21 August 2012), *Jiji Press*, http://jen.jiji.com/jc/eng?g=eco&k=2012082100864, date accessed 22 August 2012. See also "Radiation 258 Times Legal Limit Found in Fish off Fukushima" (22 August 2012), *The Asahi Shimbun*, http://ajw.asahi.com/article/0311disaster/fukushima/AJ201208220077, date accessed 23 August 2012.
190   "TEPCO (15 March 2013), *Jiji Press*, http://jen.jiji.com/jc/eng?g=eco&k=2013031501020, date accessed 17 March 2013.
191   "Cesium up to 100 Times Levels before Disaster Found in Plankton Far off Nuke Plant" (3 April 2012), *The Mainichi*, http://mdn.mainichi.jp/mdnnews/news/20120403p2a00m0na009000c.html, date accessed 3 April 2012.
192   "Researchers Find High Cesium in Some Pacific Plankton" (22 May 2013), *The Japan Times*, http://www.japantimes.co.jp/news/2013/05/22/national/researchers-find-high-cesium-in-some-pacific-plankton/#.UZ6W6ZwQNX9, date accessed 23 May 2013.
193   P. Povinec, K. Hirose, and M. Aoyama (18 September 2012) "Radiostrontium in the Western North Pacific: Characteristics, Behavior, and the Fukushima Impact," *Environmental Science and Technology*, 46.18, 10356–10363.
194   Casacuberta et al., "90Sr and 89Sr in Seawater off Japan," p. 2053.

DOI: 10.1057/9781137343123

195   K. Buesseler and Michio Aoyama (no date) "Fukushima Derived
       Radionuclides in the Ocean," http://webcache.googleusercontent.com/
       search?q=cache:qdduWwTbZ-oJ:www.whoi.edu/fileserver.do%3Fid%3D
       138584%26pt%3D2%26p%3D141569+&cd=5&hl=en&ct=clnk&gl=us, date
       accessed 14 February 2013.

196   S. Manley and C. Lowe (6 March 2012) "Canopy-Forming Kelps as
       California's Coastal Dosimeter: 131I from Damaged Japanese Reactor
       Measured in Macrocystis Pyrifera," *Environmental Science and Technology*,
       http://pubs.acs.org/doi/abs/10.1021/es203598r?journalCode=esthag, date
       accessed 7 March 2012.

197   "Study Finds Radioactive Fallout in California Kelp Beds" (5 April 2012),
       Everything Long Beach, http://www.everythinglongbeach.com/study-
       finds-radioactive-fallout-in-california-kelp-beds/, date accessed
       6 April 2012.

198   E. Behrens, F. Schwarzkopf, J. Lübbecke, and C. Böning (2012) "Model
       Simulations on the Long-Term Dispersal of ^{137}Cs Released into the Pacific
       Ocean off Fukushima," *Environmental Research Letters*, 7.3, http://iopscience.
       iop.org/1748-9326/7/3/034004/,,date accessed 1 January 2013.

199   B. Jaeschke and C. Bradshaw (January 2013) "Bioaccumulation of Tritiated
       Water in Phytoplankton and Trophic Transfer of Organically Bound
       Tritium to the Blue Mussel, Mytilus Edulis," *Journal of Environmental
       Radioactivity*, 115, 28–33.

200   "World's Oceans in 'Shocking' Decline" (20 June, 2011), *BBC*, http://www.
       bbc.co.uk/news/science-environment-13796479, date accessed 19 November
       2012.

201   B. Hönisch et al. (March 2012) "The Geological Record of Ocean
       Acidification," *Science*, 2, 1058–1063.

202   GESAMP Joint Group of Experts on the Scientific Aspects of Marine
       Environmental Protection (November 2009) "Pollution in the Open
       Ocean: A Review of Assessments and Related Studies," http://www.gesamp.
       org/data/gesamp/files/media/Publications/Reports_and_studies_79/
       gallery_1060/object_1060_large.pdf, p. 32, date accessed 30 November 2011

203   E. Landau (17 March 2011) "West Coast Officials, Obama: Don't Worry
       about Radiation Risk n U.S.," *CNN*, http://articles.cnn.com/2011–03–17/
       us/nuclear.concerns_1_potassium-iodide-radiation-levels-radioactive-
       material?_s=PM:UShttp://www.americanprogress.org/issues/2009/02/pdf/
       recession_poverty.pdf, date accessed 18 March 2011.

204   J. Favole and T. Tracy (15 March 2011) "Obama Stands by Nuclear Power,"
       The Wall Street Journal, A13.

205   Favole and Tracy "Obama Stands by Nuclear Power."

206   R. Hotz and J. Levitz (29 March 2011) "Radiation Detected in U.S.," *The Wall
       Street Journal*, A12.

DOI: 10.1057/9781137343123

207 "Radioactive Dust from Fukushima Plant Hit N. America Soon after Meltdown: Researchers" (23 June 2011), *The Mainichi*, http://mdn.mainichi.jp/mdnnews/news/20110623p2a00m0na006000c.html, date accessed 24 June 2011.

208 "Japan TV: Fukushima Radioactive Plume is Circling Earth Every 40 Days – Fallout Still Showing Spikes (VIDEO)," (27 September 2012), *Enenews* http://enenews.com/japan-tv-fukushima-radioactive-plume-is-circling-earth-every-40-days-fallout-still-spiking-this-summer-video, date accessed 27 September 2012; Source: Tohoku Broadcasting Company, Uploaded by: guardianofmiyagi.

209 L. Landau (17 March 2011) "West Coast Officials, Obama: Don't Worry about Radiation Risk in U.S.," *CNN*, http://www.cnn.com/2011/US/03/17/nuclear.concerns/index.html, date accessed 17 March 2011. Also see C. Smith (11 August 2011) "Citizen Group Wants Radiation Tests Done in Canada Following Fukushima Nuclear Disaster," *Straight.com*, http://www.straight.com/article-419976/vancouver/group-wants-radiation-tests, date accessed 11 August 2011.

210 Nuclear engineer Arnie Gundersen of Fairewinds Associates reports in interview with Chris Martenson (3 June 2011) "Protecting Yourself if the Situation Worsens Part 2," *The Martenson Report*, http://www.chrismartenson.com/martensonreport/part-2-arnie-gundersen-interview-protecting-yourself-if-situation-worsens, date accessed 3 June 2011. The research on hot particle detections was presented in a research paper by M. Kaltofen (31 October 2011) "Radiation Exposure to the Population in Japan after the Earthquake," *American Public Health Association*, http://apha.confex.com/apha/139am/webprogram/Paper254015.html, date accessed 3 June 2011

211 J. McIntyre, S. Biegalski, T. Bowyer, M. Copper, P. Eslinger, J. Hayes, D. Haas, H. Miley, J. Rishel, and V. Woods (2011) "US Particulate and Xenon Measurements Made Following the Fukushima Reactor Accident," http://www.batan.go.id/inge2011/file/day1/1650_mcintyre.pdf, date accessed 1 Janaury 2012

212 J. McMahon (27 April 2012) "Inspector General Faults EPA Radiation Monitoring," *Forbes*, http://www.forbes.com/sites/jeffmcmahon/2012/04/27/inspector-general-faults-epa-radiation-monitoring/, date accessed 27 April 2012.

213 U.S. Nuclear Regulatory Commission (17 March 2011) "Official Transcript of Proceedings of Japan's Fukushima Daiichi ET Audio File," http://pbadupws.nrc.gov/docs/ML1205/ML12052A109.pdf, p. 187, date accessed 5 November 2012.

214 H. Caldicott (April 2013) "Obama Approves Raising Permissible Levels of Nuclear Radiation in Drinking Water. Civilian Cancer Deaths Expected to Skyrocket," *Global Research*, http://www.globalresearch.ca/obama-approves-raising-permissible-levels-of-nuclear-radiation-in-drinking-water-civilian-cancer-deaths-expected-to-skyrocket/5331224, date accessed 26 April 2013.

DOI: 10.1057/9781137343123

215   J. Mangano and J. Sherman (2012) "An Unexpected Mortality Increase in the United States Following Arrival of the Radioactive Plume from Fukushima: Is There a Correlation?" *International Journal of Health Services*, 42.1, 47–62.

216   Cited in A. Cockburn (17 June 2011) "Post-Fukushima Infant Deaths in the Pacific Northwest," *Counterpunch*, http://www.counterpunch.org/cockburn06172011.html, date accessed 17 June 2011.

217   J. J. Mangano and J. D. Sherman (March 2013) "Elevated Airborne Beta Levels in Pacific/West Coast US States and Trends in Hypothyroidism among Newborns after the Fukushima Nuclear Meltdown," *Open Journal of Pediatrics*, 3, 1–9.

218   K. Grossman (16 June 2011) "Fukushima and the Nuclear Establishment," *Counterpunch*, http://counterpunch.org/grossman06162011.html, date accessed 17 June 2011.

219   R. Edwards (30 June 2011) "Revealed: British Government's Plan to Play down Fukushima," *The Guardian*, http://www.guardian.co.uk/environment/2011/jun/30/british-government-plan-play-down-fukushima, date accessed 31 June 2011.

220   Ohmae "Lessons of Fukushima Dai-ichi."

221   D. Flory (5 May 2011) "Speech, IAEA Deputy Director General and Head of Department of Nuclear Safety and Security in Vienna, Austria, 5 May 2011" *YouTube*, http://www.youtube.com/watch?v=dVLIFBQw4w0, date accessed 8 August 2011.

222   M. Obe (4 July 2012) "Fukushima Watch: At Fukushima Daini, It's Safer Inside Than Outside," *The Wall Street Journal*, http://blogs.wsj.com/japanrealtime/2012/07/04/fukushima-watch-at-fukushima-daini-its-safer-inside-than-outside/, date accessed 5 July 2012.

223   "TABLE-Japan Nuclear Plant Ops (Tokai Daini under Repair until Aug)" (12 October 2011), *Reuters*, http://af.reuters.com/article/energyOilNews/idAFL3E7L41DL20111012, date accessed 13 October 2011.

224   "Low-Level Radioactive Water Leaks at Tokai Nuclear Plant" (19 March 2012), *Kyodo News*, http://english.kyodonews.jp/news/2012/03/147881.html, date accessed 20 March 2012 and "Research Reactor Ceiling Catches Fire" (21 December 2011), *Japan Times*, http://www.japantimes.co.jp/text/nn20111221b3.html, date accessed 22 December 2011.

225   These releases were visible on the TEPCO webcam, available at http://www.TEPCO.co.jp/nu/f1-np/camera/index-j.html, dates accessed June 2011 until present. I witnessed the releases in real time on the webcam and saved screen shots documenting releases.

226   T. Sugimoto (24 July 2012) "After 500 days, Fukushima No. 1 Plant Still Not Out of the Woods," *The Asahi Shimbun*, http://ajw.asahi.com/article/0311disaster/fukushima/AJ201207240087, date accessed 25 July 2012.

DOI: 10.1057/9781137343123

227   S. Kimura and A. Hatano (4 October 2012) "Scientists in Groundbreaking Study on Effects of Radiation in Fukushima," *The Asahi Shimbun*, http://ajw.asahi.com/article/0311disaster/fukushima/AJ201210040003, date accessed 6 October 2012.

228   N. I. Ryabokon, I. I. Smolich, V. Kudryashov, and R. Goncharova (2005) "Long-Term Development of Radionuclide Exposure of Murine Rodent Populations in Belarus after the Chernobyl accident," *Radiation and Environmental Biophysics*, 44, 169–181.

229   A. Moller, A. Hagiwara, S. Matsui, S. Kasahara, K. Kawatsu, I. Nishiumi, H. Suzuki, K. Ueda, and A. Mousseau (2012) "Abundance of Birds in Fukushima as Judged from Chernobyl," *Environmental Pollution*, 164, 36–39.

230   A. Hiyama, C. Nohara, S. Kinjo, W. Taira, S. Gima, A. Tanahara, and J. Otaki (2012) "The Biological Impacts of the Fukushima Nuclear Accident on the Pale Grass Blue Butterfly," *Scientific Reports*, 1–10.

231   N. Crumpton (13 August 2012) "Severe Abnormalities Found in Fukushima Butterflies," *BBC*, http://www.bbc.co.uk/news/science-environment-19245818, date accessed 14 August 2012.

232   N. I. Ryabokon and R. Goncharova (2006) "Transgenerational Accumulation of Radiation in Small Mammals Chronically Exposed to Chernobyl Fallout," *Radiation and Environmental Biophysics*, 45, 167–177, p. 167.

233   A. Moller and T. A. Mousseau (2006) "Biological Consequences of Chernobyl: 20 Years after the Disaster," *Trends in Ecology & Evolution*, 21, 200–2007.

234   A. Moller, I. Nishiumi, H. Suzuki, K. Ueda, and T. A. Mousseau (2013) "Differences in Effects of Radiation of Animals in Fukushima and Chernobyl," *Ecological Indicators*, 24, 75–81.

235   "Government to Study Genetic Effects of Radiation" (31 August 2012), *NHK*, http://www3.nhk.or.jp/daily/english/20120831_14.html, date accessed 9 September 2012.

236   A. Matsumura (3 April 2012) "Fukushima Daiichi Site: Cesium-137 is 85 Times Greater Than at Chernobyl Accident," *Akio Matsumura: Finding the Missing Link*, http://akiomatsumura.com/2012/04/682.html, date accessed 20 April 2012.

237   The letter "Urgent Request to UN Secretary General Ban Ki-moon May 1, 2012" was released publicly and was made available at *Reader Supported News*, http://readersupportednews.org/off-site-news-section/209–209/11240-urgent-request-for-un-intervention-to-stabilize-fukushima-unit-4-spent-nuclear-fuel-, date accessed 1 May 2012.

238   Matsumura (30 April 2013) "Take Action at Fukushima: An Open Letter to Secretary General Ban Ki-moon," *Akio Matsumura: Finding the Missing Link*,

DOI: 10.1057/9781137343123

http://akiomatsumura.com/2013/04/take-action-at-fukushima-an-open-letter-to-secretary-general-ban-ki-moon.html, date accessed 19 May 2013.

239   A. Matsumura (30 April 2013) "Take Action at Fukushima: An Open Letter to Secretary General Ban Ki-moon," *Akio Matsumura: Finding the Missing Link*, http://akiomatsumura.com/2013/04/take-action-at-fukushima-an-open-letter-to-secretary-general-ban-ki-moon.html, date accessed 19 May 2013.

240   "Yastel Yamada: The Skilled Veterans Corps for Fukushima" (2012) *TUC RADIO*, http://www.tucradio.org/, http://www.tucradio.org/new.html, date accessed 30 December 2012.

241   Dr. Junro FUSE, Internist and head of Kosugi Medical Clinic near Tokyo, Japan (in Japanese with English interpretation) "Archive Footage of the NYC Press Conference May 4th 2012." *Cinema Forum Fukushima*, http://cinemaforumfukushima.org/2012/05/06/archive-footage-of-the-nyc-press-conference-may-4th-2012/On May 4, 2012, date accessed 18 May 2012.

242   "Archive Footage of the NYC Press Conference May 4th 2012," *Cinema Forum Fukushima*, http://cinemaforumfukushima.org/2012/05/06/archive-footage-of-the-nyc-press-conference-may-4th-2012/, date accessed 18 May 2012.

243   19 July 2011 meeting held by government officials with Fukushima citizens in Corasse Fukushima, Fukushima City uploaded to *YouTube*. The video is titled "Japanese Government Killing Its Own People in Fukushima" (19 July 2011), *YouTube*, https://www.youtube.com/watch?v=rVuGwc9dlhQ, date accessed 25 July 2011.

244   "1,324 Fukushima Citizens File Criminal Complaint Against TEPCO, Gov't." (12 June 2012), *Japan Today*, http://www.japantoday.com/category/crime/view/over-1300-fukushima-citizens-file-criminal-complaint-against-TEPCO, date accessed 13 June 2012.

245   "Diet Panel to Tackle Question: Did TEPCO Want to Desert Fukushima Plant?" (16 May 2012) *The Asahi Shimbun*, http://ajw.asahi.com/article/0311disaster/fukushima/AJ201205160096, date accessed 17 May 2012.

246   T. Nose and Y. Oiwa (12 September 2012) "Thyroid Tests for Fukushima Children Find No Effects from Accident," *The Asahi Shimbun*, http://ajw.asahi.com/article/0311disaster/fukushima/AJ201209120067, date accessed 13 September 2012.

247   "Fukushima Survey Lists 12 Confirmed, 15 Suspected Thyroid Cancer Cases" (5 June 2013), *Kyodo*, http://english.kyodonews.jp/news/2013/06/228639.html, date accessed 5 June 2013.

248   T. Iwata (24 November 2011) "TEPCO: Radioactive Substances Belong to Landowners, Not Us," *The Asahi Shimbun*, http://ajw.asahi.com/article/0311disaster/fukushima/AJ201111240030, date accessed 25 November 2011.

DOI: 10.1057/9781137343123

249 X. Vasquez-Maignan (2011) "Fukushima Liability and Compensation," *Nuclear Law Bulletin*, 2.88, 61–64.

250 Ex-SKF (27 January 2013) "Fukushima I Nuke Accident: TEPCO to Limit the Right to Claim Compensation to 3 Years after All," *The Mainichi*, http://mainichi.jp/feature/20110311/news/20130110ddeo41040051000c. html, date accessed 30 January 2013. Article cited by EX-SKF in *Nikkei Shinbun* 16 January 2013, http://www.nikkei.com/article/DGXNASDD1600S_ W3A110C1EB2000/, date accessed 29 January 2013.

251 T. Uranaka (8 March 2012) "Japan Lenders Ready to Back Fukushima Operator TEPCO, but Wary," *Reuters*, http://uk.reuters.com/ article/2012/03/08/japan-TEPCO-banks-idUKL4E8E80MN20120308, date accessed 8 March 2012.

252 K. Ohira and M. Fujisaki (31 July 2012) "Taxpayers, Electricity Users Finance TEPCO Bailout," *The Asahi Shimbun*, http://ajw.asahi.com/article/0311disaster/ fukushima/AJ201207310068, date accessed 9 August 2012.

253 "Oi Prompts Domestic, U.S. Antinuclear Rallies" (24 June 2012), *Japan Today*, http://www.japantimes.co.jp/text/nn20120624a4.html#.T-irZvX5Ak4, date accessed 25 June 2012.

254 S. Knight (1 February 2012) "Nuclear Safety Advisers Slam Stress Tests," *The Asahi Shimbun*, http://ajw.asahi.com/article/0311disaster/fukushima/ AJ201202010057, date accessed 2 February 2012.

255 "Abe Government Questions 'No Nuke' Future Hours after Taking Office" (28 December 2012), *The Asahi Shimbun*, http://ajw.asahi.com/article/0311disaster/ fukushima/AJ201212280059, date accessed 29 December 2012.

256 Cited and translated by Mochizuki (September 2012) "Minister of Defense: Nuclear Power Plants Give Us Deterrent Force," *Fukushima Diary*, http://fukushima-diary.com/2012/09/minister-of-defense-nuclear- plants-give-us-deterrent-force/ date accessed 30 September 2012 Original source: Minister of Defense, Satoshi Morimoto, "Nuclear plants give us deterrent force" quoted from interview "Before becoming defense minister, gave a lecture on 'deterrent capability to neighboring countries' maintain primary," http://www.47news.jp/CN/201209/ CN2012090501001977.html. Translated by Google translator, date accessed 7 October 2012.

257 H. Hattori (28 December 2012) "Nuclear Watchdog to Urge Shutdown of Oi Plant if Active Fault Found," *The Asahi Shimbun*, http://ajw.asahi.com/ article/0311disaster/fukushima/AJ201212280036, date accessed 29 December 2012.

258 "Nuclear Watchdog Execs Held 30 Illicit Meetings with Power Firms" (10 February 2013), *Japan Times*, http://www.japantimes.co.jp/news/2013/02/10/ national/exec-at-japans-nuclear-watchdog-held-30-illicit-meetings-with- power-firms/#.URcXJWf_6ul, date accessed 12 February 2013.

DOI: 10.1057/9781137343123

259 J. Solomon and M. Inada (2 May 2013) "Japan's Nuclear Plan Unsettles US," *The Wall Street Journal*, A9.

260 K. Hasegawa (19 December 2012) "Quake Risk at Japan Atomic Recycling Plant: Experts," *Pys.Org*, http://phys.org/news/2012–12-quake-japan-atomic-recycling-experts.html#jCp, date accessed 7 January 2013.

261 *H. Takashi and C. Lummis (23 May 2011), "The Nuclear Disaster That Could Destroy Japan," The Asia-Pacific Journal, 9.21(2),* http://japanfocus.org/-Hirose-Takashi/3534, date accessed 30 May 2011.

262 Ohira and Fujisaki, "Taxpayers, Electricity Users Finance TEPCO Bailout."

263 See W. Binford (February 2012) "Fallout from Fukushima: Nuclear Contamination and the Environmental Rights of Children," Lessons of Fukushima Conference, Willamette University Law School, Oregon, http://www.willamette.edu/events/fukushima/stream/index.html, date accessed 15 March 2012.

264 M. IIzuka (12 July 2012) "A-Bomb Doctor Warns of Further Fukushima Woes," *Japan Times*, http://www.japantimes.co.jp/text/nn20120712f3.html#.T_-lU_Vojwl, date accessed 14 July 2012, and "Bomb Survivor Doctor Continues to Speak up about Significance of Internal Exposure" (23 January 2012), *The Mainichi*, http://mdn.mainichi.jp/mdnnews/news/20120123p2a00m0na013000c.html, date accessed 24 January 2012.

265 IIzuka "A-Bomb Doctor Warns."

266 E. Warmerdam (26 December 2012) "U.S. Sailors Sue Japan over Fukushima," *Courthouse News Service*, http://www.courthousenews.com/2012/12/26/53414.htm, date accessed 27 December 2012.

267 T. Nakagawa (3 February 2012) "Japan Wants in on Nuclear Accident Compensation Pact," *The Asahi Shimbun*, http://ajw.asahi.com/article/behind_news/politics/AJ201202030021, date accessed 5 February 2012.

268 U. Beck cited H. Ohno (7 July 2011) "Interview/ Ulrich Beck: System of Organized Irresponsibility Behind the Fukushima Crisis," *The Asahi Shimbun*, http://www.asahi.com/english/TKY201107060307.html, date accessed 7 July 2011.

269 Beck cited in Ohno "Interview/Ulrich Beck."

DOI: 10.1057/9781137343123

4
Radiation Effects

Abstract: *Exposure to radiation increases risks for a range of diseases and genetic disorders. Yet, precise dose effects are difficult to predict with certainty because of the complexity of modeling bio-accumulation and bio-magnification processes and because of the historic Cold-War politics of a "permissible dose." Consequently, extant dose-effects models may underrepresent genomic risks from bio-accumulation, bio-magnification, and from individual and developmental susceptibilities.*

Keywords: permissible dose; 1956 BEAR Report, reference man, ICRP, Chernobyl, childhood cancer, genomic instability

Holmer Nadesan, Majia. *Fukushima and the Privatization of Risk.* Basingstoke: Palgrave Macmillan, 2013. DOI: 10.1057/9781137343123.

What are the expected health outcomes of the Fukushima nuclear disaster? There are no definitive answers to this question. Linking environmental exposures to disease symptoms is always complicated due to the range of potential variables involved and because it is challenging to prove a variable is causal, not simply correlative. The uncertainty about the actual total and ongoing emissions from the plant further complicates projections of effects. Finally, the dose-models used to predict radiation effects are themselves tentative and disputed.

There is scientific consensus that radiation exposure poses health risks, but debate exists over the short-term and long-term effects from exposure levels. Controversy also exists over whether the effects of ingested and inhaled radioisotopes are similar to the effects of exposure to gamma radiation from sources external to the body. For example, are the long-term effects from exposure to gamma radiation (e.g., from the sun) comparable or different from the long-term effects of radioactive decay from an ingested radioisotope such as uranium -235? This chapter explains debates about the types of radiation and their effects in order to fully understand the short- and long-term risks from radiation exposure, drawing implications for the Fukushima disaster.

Given the complexity of this discussion, it is helpful to identify the central actors and key debates in radiation safety before providing a more detailed narrative of research findings across time. After orienting the reader, the chapter briefly chronicles the history of "radiation risk " as it has been constructed in experimental and epidemiological research on radioisotopes since the early twentieth century, in order to demonstrate the push for nuclear weapons and energy privatized radiation-related health and reproductive risks, shifting them to the public. Women and children, whom are more vulnerable to low-dose effects, have shouldered even more risk than adult males. The chapter uses the U.S. Academy of Sciences' (1956) *Biological Effects of Atomic Radiation: A Report to the Public from a Study by The National Academies of Science* to demonstrate that geneticists warned decades ago of the potential for significant intergenerational health and reproductive risks from nuclear weapons and energy sourced radiation exposure, but their warnings were discounted because of the tests' perceived national security benefits.[1] Highly charged debates on radiation effects have prevailed since that time.

DOI: 10.1057/9781137343123

Central debates about radiation safety

In general, there are three main types of players most visible in public debates about radiation safety. First, there are national and international governmental agencies tasked with nuclear regulation and safety. The first international regulatory agency was the IAEA, established in 1957 after 81 nations approved the IAEA Statute.[2] The statute outlines the agency's three responsibilities: "nuclear verification and security, safety and technology transfer." The regulatory work conducted by the IAEA is, in principle, informed by published research on radiation safety. National regulatory agencies exist in nations with nuclear energy, including Nuclear and Industrial Safety Agency (NISA) in Japan, which prevailed from 2001 to 2012, when the Nuclear Regulation Authority (NRA) was formed.

The second group of actors in the debates about radiation safety includes national and international organizations, usually comprised of academics making policy recommendations about the relative safety of exposure levels. United Nations Scientific Committee of the Effects of Atomic Radiation (UNSCEAR), established in 1955 as a watchdog for the IAEA,[3] illustrates an international organization of this kind. UNSCEAR's mandate entails assessing and reporting levels and effects of exposure to ionizing radiation.[4] Another international organization is the International Committee on Radiation Protection (ICRP). Since 1928, the ICRP has maintained the "International System of Radiological Protection" used as a common basis for developing radiological protection standards and legislations. Many nations have national equivalents of the ICRP (e.g., U.S. NCRP).

A related source of recommendations on radiation comes from nongovernmental national and international science academies. In Europe today, an independent and expert committee, the European Commission on Radiological Protection (ECRP), makes its own recommendations for radiological protection based on some differences with the ICRP in interpreting dose effects, particularly for internal emitters. The US Academy of Sciences issued one, if not *the*, first independent and public reports on radiation effects from atmospheric testing : the 1956 *Biological Effects of Atomic Radiation: A Report to the Public from a Study by the National Academy of Sciences* (BEAR). The U.S. BEAR report will be featured in this chapter, as its warnings about the long-term genomic effects of radiation exposure were prescient in many ways.

DOI: 10.1057/9781137343123

The third group of actors visible in public debates on radiation safety is a diverse assortment of independent scientists and activists. Although many scientists quietly study and publish on effects of radiation, this chapter's discussion will primarily focus on two vocal and opposed groups: (1) those with "pro-nuclear" research funded by the nuclear industry and/or pro-nuclear government agencies, and (2) those with "anti-nuclear" research funded by environmental organizations, such as Greenpeace, or conducted entirely independently.

The various actors outlined above are contenders in the playing field of radiation safety. One important debate in radiation safety concerns the legitimacy of the linear, no-threshold model, which holds there is no safe level of exposure for any additional increments of radiation beyond zero exposure. At issue in this first debate is the definition for the "threshold" of harm for long-term effects, as well as the methods and means for documenting harm.

The official stance of most regulatory and research agencies holds that there exists a "linear, no-threshold dose-response relationship between exposure to ionizing radiation and the development of cancer in humans."[5] In practice, most nations set "permissible dose" levels for exposure to radiation. For instance, the United Kingdom adopts the ALARP, that is "as low as reasonably practicable" cost-benefit system and the United States, in principle, adopts ALARA, that is "as low as reasonably achievable."[6] However, national regulatory agencies typically have discretion in operationalizing "as low as reasonably achievable."

Debate typically focuses on determining precise-dose effects from various forms of radiation in order to calculate risks when setting standards for permissible dose. The ICRP attempted to simplify this process in 1977 by creating a "reference man" to calculate the excess risks for fatal cancer caused by exposure to radiation.[7] The reference man was defined as a Caucasian man between 20 and 30 years of age, weighing approximately 154 pounds. The model was offered as basis for setting regulatory exposure guidelines despite the fact that it homogenizes the population, preventing consideration of effects on more vulnerable populations. The 2006 U.S. National Academies' panel on the risks of low-level radiation, the Biological Effects of Ionizing Radiation (BEIR) VII report, found that overall fatal cancer risk for females was 37.5 percent greater than for males exposed to the same radiation dose, and children are even more vulnerable.[8] Despite these findings, the reference man continues to inform many international and national regulatory guidelines, including the ICRP.[9]

DOI: 10.1057/9781137343123

As illustrated by this example, there exists considerable debate about the validity of dose-effect models because of the complexities surrounding their development. There are many types of evidence that can be used to develop predictions of excess risks for disease, birth defects, and subtle biological changes posed by exposure to ionizing radiation. Epidemiological data can be collected on populations known to have exposure to radioisotopes. Studies have been conducted on many different populations, including those exposed to atmospheric testing in the 1950s and early 1960s, as well as those exposed to the Chernobyl disaster. Studies can also be conducted on animals accidently or deliberately exposed to various types of radiation in "the field" or in labs. Laboratory research can take a more micro focus and investigate the effects on DNA in cells after exposures to radiation. Innovations in assays now allow scientists in labs to study microscopically how cellular reproduction is affected across time by radiation exposure. Assembling all of the diverse findings into a unified body of knowledge informing safety protocols is challenging methodologically and politically. So, models used by organizations such as the ICRP are slow to change.

One particularly hot debate across research approaches is whether low doses can be extrapolated from the effects of high doses. The linear no-threshold model, informing dose-effect calculations, presumes that the effects from low doses can be predicted from the effects of high doses. Yet, new research on chemicals and radiation reveals that in some instances dose effects do not follow linear models. For instance, endocrine disruptors (chemicals found in plastics, cosmetics, etc.) can have significant effects across a range of doses and large effects can be seen from small doses during vulnerable times in development.[10] An epidemiological study of Chernobyl effects, by Jay M. Gould and Benjamin A. Goldman, found a "supralinear" dose-response effect for infants, meaning infant mortality rose more rapidly at low doses of exposure.[11] Gene-environment interactions are probably not simply linear and additive, but rather are likely complex, synergistic, and developmentally contingent.

Another heated debate concerns the dose effects of internal emitters versus external exposure to radiation. The 2006 BEIR report notes that ingested alpha emitters (e.g., uranium and plutonium) are more effective than low linear energy transfer (LET) radiation (e.g., gamma rays) in producing genomic instability.[12] Yet, the report concludes, "How this translates into risks of late effects in man is

DOI: 10.1057/9781137343123

an open question."[13] The ICRP addresses this problem by averaging the radiation dose produced by an ingested alpha particle across the entirety of the impacted organ when calculating the "absorbed dose" in relation to subsequent cancer risks. In contrast, some critics, such as those promoting the ECRP model, contend that the dose effects from ingestion of radioisotopes should be examined in terms of their more narrowly focused effects on directly targeted and bystander cells.[14] The ECRP model predicts greater genetic damage from internally ingested radioisotopes due to targeted effects. Both approaches emphasize clinical cell death over the subtle genomic instabilities that exert deleterious, delayed influences – including germ line instabilities – now being studied in laboratory research.

Laboratory and epidemiological research findings are political because they raise questions about the liability of polluters and the necessity of regulation. Therefore, debates about the dose effects of low-level radiation and ingested radioisotopes are slow to be resolved and are even more slowly incorporated into formal exposure guidelines. Exposure guidelines therefore offer some, but inherently limited, protection from health risks caused by exposure to radioisotopes.

It is instructive to note that even the most stringent regulatory standards are often based on risk coefficient tables that presume risk can be predicted on the basis of exposure to a single radionuclide. For example:

> For both internal and external exposure, a risk coefficient for a given radionuclide is based on the assumption that this is the only radionuclide present in the environmental medium. That is, doses due to decay chain members produced in the environment prior to the intake of, or external exposure to, the radionuclides are not considered.[15]

This model of dose effects taken from the U.S. Environmental Protection Agency (EPA) assumes a vacuum where exposure is limited to a single radionuclide. The model's predictions for dose effects do not incorporate cumulative and synergistic effects.

Real-world chemical and radiation effects for flora and fauna are impacted by bio-accumulation and exposure interactions. Bio-accumulation is "the biological sequestering of a substance at a higher concentration than that at which it occurs in the surrounding environment or medium."[16] Bio-magnification is defined as "the sequence of processes in an ecosystem by which higher concentrations of a particular

DOI: 10.1057/9781137343123

chemical, such as the pesticide DDT, are reached in organisms higher up the food chain, generally through a series of prey-predator relationships." Bio-magnification results from bio-accumulation and biotransfer whereby "tissue concentrations of chemicals in organisms at one trophic level exceed tissue concentrations in organisms at the next lower trophic level in a food chain."[17]

Takashi Hirose provides an example of the implications of bio-magnification processes in his book, *Fukushima Meltdown*, using actual radioactivity concentration data from the Columbia River: The egg yolk of a water bird living by the Columbia river near Hanford would contain 1,000,000 more radiation than the river water because of bio-accumulation and bio-magnification processes.[18] Humans that consume meat, milk, and eggs are at the top of the food chain and therefore will accumulate significant levels of contamination over the course of their lifetime. The impact of biocontamination is also affected synergistically by the presence of other radioisotopes and chemicals. It can be difficult to predict exposure interactions given the complex synergies of bio-accumulation processes.

Genetic damage and epigenetic changes to gene expression can be transmitted across generations. Each person inherits the totality of genetic damage and epigenetic changes to their parents' germ-line, or reproductive cells. Consequently, even the most precautionary risk assessments from agencies such as the ICRP may understate real-world risks from exposure by failing to account for cumulative and synergistic effects.

What follows is a selective chronology of research findings across time on the biological effects of radiation. The chronology focuses on how risks from ionizing radiation were "discovered" and debated across the twentieth century. It reveals that many of the scientific pioneers who discovered radiation were often sickened from their exposure. Likewise, the incorporation of radiation into consumer products and health practices frequently produced more damage than benefits for consumers and patients. Yet, increasing knowledge about radiation risks coincided with the buildup to World War II. The importance attached to nuclear weapons during World War II and the Cold War had the effect of prioritizing weapons and energy research over the potential biological risks for populations exposed to radiation emissions.

DOI: 10.1057/9781137343123

Atomic energy: discovery, deployment, research

Ionizing radiation refers to a range of phenomena, including beta and alpha particles, and gamma and X-rays.[19] Gamma and x-rays are part of the electromagnetic spectrum and have strong penetrating power. Beta particles are high-speed, negatively charged electrons and positions that move close to the speed of light. Alpha particles are composed of two protons and two neutrons. Alpha and beta particles are emitted by the decay of unstable atoms, such as isotopes of uranium. These diverse phenomena of ionizing radiation are grouped on their capacity to dislodge an electron from an atom. Biological damage can result from the electron discharge as chemical bonds are broken. Those who discovered ionizing radiation at the close of the nineteenth century did not immediately understand the hazards of their findings. However, by the end of the 1930s it was clear to all, at least in the United States and Europe, that high-frequency electromagnetic radiation such as X-rays and gamma rays cause cancer and that ingested radioisotopes such as radium-226 are deadly poisons.

Discovery of radiation forms

Discovery of high-frequency electromagnetic radiation known as X-rays is traced to Wilhelm Röntgen's work in the late nineteenth century. Röntgen discovered X-rays in 1895 while conducting experiments with electrical discharge tubes.[20] Not knowing their nature, he referred to them as "X" rays. He published his findings in scientific proceedings, but the X-ray image he had produced of his wife's hand was disseminated extensively in popular media.[21] X-rays were determined to be electromagnetic waves in 1912 by Max von Laue.[22]

X-rays soon captivated the public imagination and were widely employed in medicine and popular culture to reveal the previously hidden internal world of the living, human skeletal system. However, medical applications (e.g., to eliminate moles) and parlor games with X-rays were soon linked with adverse health effects, including burns. J. Samuel Walker notes in *Permissible Dose* that within two decades of their discovery in 1895, X-rays had been linked to skin burns, bone disease, and cancer.[23]

Henri Becquerel encouraged research on a different type of ray, the "Becquerel ray," when he discovered in 1896 that uranium salts could fog a photographic plate without excitation by an external energy source

DOI: 10.1057/9781137343123

such as sunlight. Paul Villard investigated the Becquerel rays produced by radium and detected what is now known as gamma radiation, which is part of the electromagnetic spectrum, but has shorter wave lengths than X-rays. Marie and Pierre Curie proposed that the Becquerel rays emitted by uranium and radium were made up of particles after Marie determined that minerals containing uranium produced a measurable electrical current in air.[24] The Curies described radioisotopes of radium and polonium, which Marie strove to isolate chemically, in order to better study their emissions. Ernest Rutherford further explicated the nature of these rays by distinguishing among those comprised of electromagnetic radiation (gamma), those composed of electrons (beta particles), and those composed of protons and neutrons (alpha particles).[25] Working with Frederick Soddy, Rutherford then proposed a mechanism for radioactive transmutation of elements, or decay, which was reported in their 1902 paper, "The Cause and Nature of Radioactivity."[26]

Like X-Rays, these new rays deriving from the decay of radioisotopes were thought to confer medical benefits. Pierre Curie suggested that rays from radium could destroy tumor cells after studying their effect on living tissue. Marie's death by leukemia caused by her radiation exposure illustrated the need for judicious assessments of dose given the rays' proven toxicity. However, enthusiasm overwhelmed prudence. By the 1920s radium was used widely in medicine to destroy cancer tumors, as a curative for tuberculosis, and a fix for skin rigidities caused by accidents.[27] Radium was added to patent medicines until it was linked to a mysterious and fatal wasting disease in the 1930s. Proof of the special toxicity posed by ingested radium was presented by the wasting illnesses and deaths of women working at the Radium Dial factory in Ottawa, Illinois who routinely licked paint brushes covered in radium paint.[28]

The power of radiation to produce biological harm caught the attention of a scientist studying chromosomal heredity. H. J. Muller used mutagenesis as a strategy for revealing the chemical nature and physical operations of hereditary. In 1926 Muller concluded that reproductive cells are particularly susceptible to X-rays:

> It has been found quite conclusively that treatment of the sperm with relatively heavy doses of X-rays induces the occurrence of true "gene mutations" in a high proportion of the treated germ cell. Several hundred mutants have been obtained in this way in a short time and considerably more than a hundred of the mutant genes have been followed through three, four, or more generations.[29]

DOI: 10.1057/9781137343123

Researchers following Muller's work found that gamma rays from radium could also produce genetic mutations.[30]

Publicity surrounding findings on the dangers of radiation eventually led to calls for international and national safety regulations. In 1928, the ICRP issued a publication on radiation safety.[31] It did not incorporate genetic findings into its recommendations; rather, it developed a tolerance dose for workers based on one-hundredth of the dose of radium believed necessary in producing visible reddening of the skin.[32] The early ICRP model presumed that an equilibrium state existed between somatic injury and repair caused by exposure to radioisotopes.[33] Proposed, but not enforceable, new guidelines by radiation protection committees did not halt the continued use of radium in homeopathic medicine.

The atomic bomb: weaponization of radiation

The race for the nuclear bomb during World War II prompted research on atomic properties and effects. In 1938 a research team in Germany discovered that shattering uranium nuclei with neutrons released large amounts of energy.[34] German, Austrian, and Danish scientists escaping persecution by the Nazis brought news of this discovery to the English-speaking scientific community in 1939. During the same year, Albert Einstein wrote a letter to Franklin D. Roosevelt outlining the practical development of an atomic bomb.[35] J. Robert Oppenheimer was delegated the responsibility of the Manhattan Project, which culminated in the atomic bombs dropped on Hiroshima and Nagasaki. This section briefly examines the research on the health effects of ionizing radiation conducted during and immediately after World War II.

The Manhattan Project research was not restricted to bomb development. Medical studies of radiation effects were also funded as part of the project. Atomic decision-makers wanted to understand the myriad ways that detonation of an atomic bomb would affect human health.

A U.S. camera crew was deployed to document the biological effects of the bomb exploded over Nagasaki. The footage was so disturbing it remained classified for decades.[36] Field research was supplemented with experimental studies in the late 1940s and 1950s addressing how inhaled and ingested radioisotopes affect biological health in animals and people (including children), as documented by Eileen Welsome in *The Plutonium Files*.[37] However, many studies were sealed and later destroyed. *In the Name of Science*, Andrew Goliszek described a classified

DOI: 10.1057/9781137343123

Atomic Energy Commission (AEC) document dated 17 April 1947, titled "Medical Experiments in Humans" that reads: "It is desired that no document be released which refers to experiments with humans that might have an adverse effect on public opinion or result in legal suits. Documents covering such field work should be classified secret."[38] In 1994, the media reported that Cold-War records of plutonium injections without consent and other human rights violations were destroyed by the CIA in 1973.[39]

Nuclear historian Paul Langley argued in *Medicine and the Bomb: Deceptions from Trinity to Maralinga* that AEC research on the health effects of radiation essentially weaponized fallout.[40] Among other sources, Langley used wartime work by Joe Hamilton to document AEC knowledge about adverse effects from radiation exposure. Hamilton's "The Metabolism of the Fission Products", presented at the 32nd Annual Meeting of the Radiological Society of North America, Chicago, Ill., 1–6 December, 1946 received government funding.[41] Hamilton's research concluded that ingestion of plutonium is significantly more damaging than external exposure to beta or gamma irradiation:

> The most important hazard that arises from the release of nuclear energy are radiations produced directly from fission and subsequently emitted by the resultant fission products and plutonium. The fission products can produce injury either as an external source of radiation or, if they gain entry into the body, by acting as an internal radioactive poison, quite analogous to radium poisoning. This latter consideration is a major concern, since the amounts required within the body to produce injurious effects are minute compared to the quantities necessary to induce damage by external beta and gamma irradiation.

Langley's analysis of wartime research demonstrates that those involved in the atomic arms race were well aware from the start that weapons' fallout would have severe health impacts on civilian populations.

From World War II forward, atomic policy makers prioritized "atomic security " through nuclear weapons development over considerations of the biological risks from their deployment. Radiation safety considerations were not permitted to impact worker progress on the Manhattan Project and two researchers died from their exposure.[42] Wartime deployment of the atomic bomb made civilian "collateral damage" unavoidable. The imperative for atmospheric testing was prioritized over risks to human health, beginning with the Trinity test in New Mexico on 16 July

DOI: 10.1057/9781137343123

1945. The imperative of atomic weapons justified using children and other populations as unwitting subjects of secret radiation experiments during World War II and through much of the Cold-War era.

The Japanese Radiation Effects Research Foundation

The Radiation Effects Research Foundation in Hiroshima was established in 1950 to study the effects of exposure on atomic bomb survivors. Fourteen studies have been published from the data collected from a cohort of approximately 120,000 subjects. The participants included residents of Hiroshima and Nagasaki, both in and outside of city, at the time of the bombing.[43] In the foundation's most recent report published in 2012, the data support the linear, no-threshold model of the effects of ionizing radiation. Moreover, their research has linked diseases beyond cancer – including circulatory, respiratory, and digestive disease – to fallout exposure. Health effects are documented at exposure levels of 20 millisieverts and a "statistically significant upward curvature" of effects for low doses is documented.[44] This upward curvature raises questions about the effects of low doses. Could there be an adverse dose-response at the low end?[45] This question permeates the scientific literature on the biological effects of radiation.

Research on the atomic bomb survivors has been the foundation of post-World War II government understandings of dose effects, excess relative risk from radiation exposure (ERR), and radiation protection regulations. However, although the atomic bomb survivors represent the largest available cohort on excessive radiation exposure, there have been four main criticisms of conducting research on atomic bomb victims. First, the research findings on atomic bomb survivors who were exposed to high doses have been used to extrapolate the effects of low doses. This strategy essentially homogenizes and incrementalizes the effects of dose. Criticisms of this practice of extrapolation have been launched by those who argue that the effects of low-level radiation are not necessarily the same as the effects of acute exposure to higher-level radiation. Second, some critics have noted that the population of survivors from the blast may not be representative of the larger population impacted by the disaster and therefore survivors may have biological predispositions enabling greater survivorship capacities. Third, critics claim the study of survivors was severely biased because many people in Japan hid symptoms of fallout exposure for fear of social exclusion and economic

DOI: 10.1057/9781137343123

marginalization.[46] Finally, critics argue that fallout effect from the atomic bombs dropped on Hiroshima and Nagasaki cannot be extrapolated to encompass all forms of radiological contamination since they were detonated at relatively high altitudes and produced minimal fallout.[47] These charges suggest effects could have been more substantial than statistical data suggest.

Atmospheric testing

Atmospheric testing, beginning in Trinity in New Mexico in 1945, constituted an unprecedented medical experiment by governments. The United States, the Soviet Union, and the United Kingdom conducted atmospheric testing until 1963 when the limited test ban treaty was signed. France and China persisted with atmospheric tests through the 1980s. In sum, 504 nuclear devices are known to have been detonated above ground.[48] The United States alone conducted a total of 1,030 atmospheric and below ground tests. The human and biosphere costs are incalculable and few governments in the world have incentives for attempting to calculate them.

Growing public concern about fallout in the 1950s produced reassurances from government authorities. After fallout from a U.S. test explosion at Bikini Atoll in March 1954 forced evacuation of Marshallese from their homes, the media reassured the international public that the health effects were transitory despite reports of hair whitening, hair loss, widespread skin lesions, and blood changes. For instance, in 1954 *The New York Times* ran an article reassuringly titled, "Fall-Out Effects Gone in 6 Months: 5 Navy Doctors Tell A.M.A: Pacific Blast Caused Mainly Skin Damage."[49] The article closed with, "Children appeared to be slightly more sensitive to radiation than adults, it was suggested." Despite this "mishap," the United Nations upheld the U.S. "right" to conduct hydrogen bomb testing in the Pacific. The petition brought forward by the Marshallese that testing be stopped was disregarded. The U.S. AEC, tasked with oversight of nuclear issues, argued that the tests were critical for U. S. security.[50]

Although the Marshallese were considered fully recovered from exposures of up to 400 roentgens after six months, the U.S. National Radiation Protection Agency recommended that in the growing nuclear energy industry, plant workers' exposure limit be set at a maximum of three-tenths of a roentgen. Professor G. Hoyt Whipple, a pathologist, was

DOI: 10.1057/9781137343123

quoted by *The New York Times* as recommending that figure be reduced to three-hundredths of a roentgen because animal experiments showed the three-tenths dosage would shorten human life expectancy by 10 percent over 30 years.[51] Whipple cautioned that the children of people exposed, and their succeeding generations, were at risk for genetic mutations. He was quoted as stating that the problem "is one of conservation – conservation of the human race if you will."

In 1954, Detlev Bronk, president of the US National Academy of Sciences, established the Committees on The Biological Effects of Atomic Radiation to conduct a thorough review of studies examining the effects of atomic radiation.[52] Research funding was provided by the Rockefeller Foundation. Committees included Pathologic Effects; Genetic Effects; Meteorological Effects; Agriculture and Food Supplies Effects; Disposal and Dispersal of Radioactive Wastes; and Oceanography and Fisheries Effects. The committees ultimately produced two public reports in 1956 and 1960, which abstracted committee findings, before the project's dissolution in 1964. Media coverage of the 1956 public report simultaneously reaffirmed and tempered public concern about the health and reproductive risks of radioactive fallout from atmospheric testing and nuclear plant accidents.

BEAR 1956

The 1956 BEAR report was issued as a 49-page summary report by the National Academy of Sciences. The report is historically important because it represents one of the earliest independent efforts to map the range of environmental and health effects of nuclear fallout from atmospheric testing. In "A Dispassionate and Objective Effort: Negotiating the First Study on the Biological Effects of Atomic Radiation" historian Jacob Hamblin argued the 1956 report was a delicate product of negotiation and that the Academy influenced coverage of findings in media outlets, including the *New York Times* and *Scientific American*.[53] Hamblin described how the AEC lobbied to have representation on committees and limited committee scientists' access to classified wartime research on the biological effects of radiation. The AEC was particularly interested in ensuring its representation on the pathology and genetics committees and successfully lobbied to place on them representatives from Oak Ridge, Argonne, and the Naval Radiation Defense laboratories.

DOI: 10.1057/9781137343123

The AEC had previously established its preferences for assessing health risks from radiation when it lobbied to have workplace exposure defined in relation to acute exposure effects in 1947.[54] In contrast, some scientists on the pathology and genetics committees rejected altogether the idea of a safe level, or "threshold" of exposure.[55] On the genetics committee, A. H. Sturtevant, of California Institute of Technology in Pasadena, subscribed to the latter position. He had previously debated permissible dose guidelines proposed by the AEC, arguing that low levels of exposure produced health and reproductive effects.[56] Sturtevant was supported by H. J. Muller, also on the genetics committee, who found the idea of a permissible "safe" dose from atmospheric testing to be problematic. Sturtevant and Miller also rejected the AEC tactic of describing radiation exposure in terms of "sunlight unit" given the documented ill effects of ingested radioisotopes. Conflict ensued because of clashing methods for measuring effects. However, in the end, the AEC scientists were simply better situated to promote their stance in relation to atmospheric testing and proposed developments in nuclear energy.[57]

The AEC influence was evident in the public report summary published in *The New York Times*, which concluded that radiation causes genetic damage, but that a threshold exists for "safe exposure." The 13 July 1956 *New York Times* (NYT) article, titled "Text of Genetics Committee Report Concerning Effects of Radioactivity on Heredity", featured six scientists: Geoffrey Norman, Harry Wexler, Detlev Bronk, Shields Warren, Abel Wolman, and Roger Revell.[58] This membership body was not identical with the actual genetics subcommittee.[59] The NYT text is similar, but not identical with, the genetics committee abstract in the actual report; however, the former includes introductory text not in the actual report. Excerpts will be taken from the NYT version because AEC influence is evident in its greater emphasis on cost-benefit analysis of atomic radiation. Yet, in spite of this influence, strong wording about the hereditary risks of radiation-induced mutations echo through the text.

The NYT "Text of Genetics Committee Report Concerning Effects of Radioactivity on Heredity" begins with by acknowledging readers' concerns:

> Are we harming ourselves and are there genetic effects which will harm our children and their descendants, through this radioactive dust that has been settling down on all of us? Are things going to be still worse when presently we have a lot of atomic power plants, more laboratories experimenting with atomic fission and fusion, and perhaps more and bigger weapons testing?

DOI: 10.1057/9781137343123

Are there similar risks, due to other sources of radiation, but brought to our attention by these atomic risks?[60]

It continues, "even very small amounts of radiation unquestionably have the power to injure hereditary materials," contending that many specific questions about precise effects cannot be answered because of the nascent state of genetic research. It advises readers that evaluation of potential risks ought also involve "a weighing of values and a balance of opposing aim," hence, "what is involved is not an elimination of all risks, for that is impossible – it is a balance of opposing risks and of different sorts of benefits." Yet, it acknowledges the imprecision that clouds rational risks assessments: "And the disturbing and confusing thing is that mankind has to seek to balance the scale, when the risk on neither side is completely visible."

After framing the issue of health effects in terms of uncertainty and cost-benefit calculi, the article proceeds to describe evolving understandings of radiation's hereditary effects. It acknowledges that committee findings were, for the most part, based on studies of bacteria, fruit flies, and mice, but emphasizes the universal chemistry of heredity, thereby legitimizing conclusions drawn for human health:

> The chemical nature of hereditary material is universally the same; the main pattern of hereditary transmission of traits is the same for all life reproducing sexually; and the nature of the effects of high energy radiations upon the genetic material is likewise universally the same in principle. Hence when it comes to human... we can at least feel certain of the general nature of the effects, and need only to discover ways in which to measure them precisely.

The article takes a pedagogical tone as it commences with a description of genes and the biological effects of their mutation by radiation:

> When a gene becomes permanently altered, we say it mutates. The gene in its altered form is then duplicated in each subsequent cell division. If the mutant gene is in an ordinary body cell, then it is merely passed along to the body cells; but the mutant gene under these circumstances, is not passed on to the progeny, and the effect of the mutant gene is limited to the person in whom the mutation occurred.

The article cautions that mutant genes pose dangers to affected individuals, including shortened life expectancy and potentially reduced fertility. However, the greatest concern is expressed over the impact on

DOI: 10.1057/9781137343123

subsequent generations when mutations occur in reproductive "germ line" cells, which are transmitted across generations. These mutations often occur in recessive genes so they may not result in overt malformations, even while they can impact the health, longevity, and fecundity of descendants:

> Of great importance for our present study is the fact that mutant genes – genes which have, for example, been changed by radiations – are usually of the recessive types. It is now easy to see that any organism may have, latent in its genetic constitution, ineffectual or recessive genes that have not had much of a chance to become apparent in its developed external characteristics since the recessive genes are masked by their dominant companion genes... Moreover the mutant genes, in the vast majority of cases, and in all the species so far studied, lead to some kind of harmful effect. In extreme cases the harmful effect is death itself, or the loss of the ability to produce offspring, or some other serious abnormality.

However, although gross abnormalities are of concern, the article notes that a more significant risk to the human population at large may be posed by genetic mutations that have less dramatic effects, at least initially: "A mildly deleterious gene may eventually do just as much total damage as a grossly and abruptly one, since the milder mutant persists longer and has a chance to harm more people." By examining the inter-generation transmission and bio-accumulation of largely recessive mutations, the article implicates the inheritance of mutated genes as a kind of hidden time bomb that can ultimately lead to an inability to procreate the human species.

The pedagogical tone is reinforced by a series of itemized conclusions briefly summarized here:

1   Radiations cause mutations. Mutations affect those hereditary traits which a person passes on to his children and subsequent generations.
2   Practically all radiation-induced mutations which have effects large enough to be detected are harmful. A small but not negligible part of this harm would appear in the first generation of the offspring of the person who received the radiation. Most of the harm, however, would remain unnoticed, for a shorter or longer time, in the genetic constitution of the successive generations of offspring. But the harm would persist, and some of it would be expressed in each generation.

DOI: 10.1057/9781137343123

3   Any radiation dose, however small, can induce some mutations. There is no minimum radiation dose, that is, which must be exceeded before any harmful mutations occur.

4   Like radiation-induced mutations, nearly all spontaneous mutations with detectable effects are harmful. Hence these mutations tend to eliminate themselves from the population through the handicaps of the tragedies which occur because the persons bearing these mutations are not ideally fit to survive.

5   Additional radiation (i.e., radiation over and above the irreducible minimum due to natural causes) produces additional mutations (over and above the spontaneous mutations).

The probable number of additional induced mutations that occur in an individual over a period of time is by and large proportional to the total dose of extra radiation received, over that period, by the reproductive organs where the germ cells are formed and stored. To the best of our present knowledge, if we increase the radiation by X percent, the gene mutations caused by radiation will also be increased by X percent.

The total dose of radiation is what counts: this statement is based on the fact that the genetic damage done by radiation is cumulative.

6   From the above five statements a very important conclusion results. It has sometimes been thought that there may be a rate (say, so much per week) at which a person can receive radiation with reasonable safety as regards certain types of direct damage to his own person. But the concept of a safe rate of radiation simply does not make sense if one is concerned with genetic damage to future generations. What counts, from the point of view of genetic damage, is not the rate; it is the total accumulated dose to the reproductive cells of the individual from the beginning of his life up to the time the child is conceived.

What is genetically important to a child is the total radiation dose that the child's parents have received from their conception to the conception of the child.

There are at least three different aspects which must be considered. The first aspect places emphasis on the risk to the direct offspring and later descendants of those persons who, from occupation hazard or otherwise, receive a radiation dose substantially greater than the average received by the population as a whole.

DOI: 10.1057/9781137343123

The second aspect refers to the effect of the average dose on the population as a whole. The third aspect refers in still broader terms to the possibility that increased and prolonged radiation must so raise the death rate and so lower the birth rate, and the population, considered as a whole, would decline and eventually perish. We are at present extremely uncertain as to the level of this fatal threshold for a human population.

The article concludes that although society may continue to promote atomic technology, "from the point of view of genetics " radiation from medical technology, atmospheric testing, and nuclear energy "are all bad."

Efforts by scientists, such as Sturtevant and Muller, to alert the public to the hereditary effects of radiation ultimately bolstered anti-nuclear activism and helped loosen the AEC hold over public policy, despite the agency's formidable power and influence. Although the cumulative effects of atmospheric testing have not been tallied, research conducted on specific populations accidentally and deliberately exposed to atmospheric testing show increased rates of cancer and reproductive issues.[61] The full effects from exposure to atmospheric fallout are still unfolding.[62]

Debating the effects of ionizing radiation: 1960s–present period

Global public concern about atmospheric testing grew across the late 1950s and early 1960s, resulting in the Limited Test Ban Treaty in 1963 by the Soviet Union and the United States. The treaty banned all atmospheric testing, restricting it to underground detonations. However, the rapid expansion of nuclear power plants and the problem of nuclear waste storage meant that the issues of radiation safety raised in the 1950s remained relevant in the 1960s and beyond. The debates about what constituted permissible doses for public exposure raged on and were exacerbated by research suggesting children's particular vulnerability. This section concludes the historical review of research on the effects of ionizing radiation by examining *in vivo* studies of the effects of ionizing radiation on people, particularly children, exposed to radiation and *in vitro* studies examining the effects of ionizing radiation on cell cultures in laboratory settings. The latter research sheds insight on "bystander" and "delayed" effects of ionizing radiation on DNA mutations. These

DOI: 10.1057/9781137343123

effects may explain why *in vivo* studies of exposure often find effects significantly in excess of those predicted by the ICRP dose model.

Children exposed to ionizing radiation

Establishing children as particularly susceptible to radiation damage required epidemiological research and public advocacy. In the late 1960s and early 1970s British epidemiologist Alice Steward of Oxford University raised awareness in her ground-breaking work on the harmful effects of X-rays on human fetal development and childhood leukemia. Children born to mothers who had X-rays during pregnancy had a 40 percent increase in incidents of leukemia and other cancers.[63] Ernest J. Sternglass followed Steward's work, publishing, "Cancer: Relation of Prenatal Radiation to Development of the Disease in Childhood," in *Science* in 1963.[64] In 1969, he publicized his research by arguing in *Esquire* magazine that radioactive fallout from atmospheric testing had caused the death of 375,000 infants less than a year old and countless fetal deaths between 1951 and 1966.[65] In 1972, Sternglass detailed his concerns about the effects of fallout in *Low-Level Radiation*, re-titled in 1981, *Secret Fallout : Low-Level Radiation from Hiroshima to Three Mile Island*.

Sternglass's argument drew controversy, although his most pointed critic, Arthur R. Tamplin, did not dispute that fallout deaths had occurred; rather, he disagreed with Sternglass about their magnitude. Tamplin calculated 8,000 fetal deaths and 4,000 infant mortalities.[66] Although Tamplin was disputing Sternglass's estimates, the AEC attempted to censor his report by asking him to withdraw his mortality calculations, fearing the public would find them alarming. Tamplin's subsequent research on the health effects of nuclear power earned him more enmity. However, he had support from John W. Goffman at Lawrence Livermore Lab where he worked. In 1969, they argued together in a research paper that annually, 17,000 additional cases of cancer would derive from the permissible *lifetime* dose of 0.17 rads per year.[67] They urged that the permissible dose be lowered. In the 1982 anti-nuclear book, *Nuclear Witnesses: Insiders Speak Out*, Goffman declared that the promises of nuclear energy were deluded: "And I realized that the entire nuclear power program was based on a fraud- namely, that there was a 'safe' amount of radiation, a permissible dose that wouldn't hurt anybody. I talked to Art Tamplin. 'They have to destroy us Art. Because they can't live with our argument that there's no safe threshold.'"[68]

DOI: 10.1057/9781137343123

To this day, conflict exists about the legitimacy of a permissible dose for guaranteeing public safety given variability in effects across populations. Research on children living in close proximity to nuclear power plants tends to support the "no safe dose" argument for susceptible populations. A study by the Institut National de la Sante et de la Recherche Medicale (French Institute of Health and Medical Research, or INSERM) documented a leukemia rate twice as high among children under the age of 15, living within a five-kilometer radius of France's 19 nuclear power plants, when compared to those living 20 kilometers or more away from a plant.[69] The French study reinforced previous findings on excess risk for leukemia in young children living in close proximity to German nuclear power plants.[70] In a commentary, "Childhood Cancer near Nuclear Power Stations," published in *Environmental Health Perspectives*, Ian Fairlie observed: "Doses from environmental emissions from nuclear reactors to embryos and fetuses in pregnant women near nuclear power stations may be larger than suspected. Hematopoietic tissues appear to be considerably more radiosensitive in embryos/fetuses than in newborn babies."[71]

Exposure to tritium may be a primary agent culpable for cancer and leukemia in children caused by nuclear power plant emissions. Water that cools reactor cores and spent fuel pools becomes extensively contaminated with tritium.[72] Tritium is a radioactive isotope of hydrogen with a half-life of 12.32 years, emitting beta particles as it decays. It is very difficult to contain and is therefore nearly continuously emitted from nuclear plants. It binds with oxygen and ends up in precipitation and water supplies, where it can be inhaled, ingested or absorbed through the skin. Harrison and Day describe the biological effects of tritium in their article "Radiation Doses and Risks from Internal Emitters":

> low energy beta emissions from tritium (3H) decay have been shown to have RBE (ratio of the absorbed dose) values of up to between 2 and 3 (compared to gamma rays), for *in vitro* end-points including cell killing, mutation and induction of chromosomal aberrations.[73]

Tritium has been linked to chromosomal breaks, brain tumors, ovarian tumors, decreased brain weight in offspring, and mental retardation in animal studies.[74] Tritium has also been found to bio-accumulate in marine species and may in land-based life as well.[75] Clyde Stagner's *Hidden Tritium* empirically examines tritium emissions from spent fuel pool evaporations in the United States, documenting how levels surpass NRC exposure guidelines.[76]

DOI: 10.1057/9781137343123

Other research has examined the health effects for children exposed to higher than ordinary gamma radiation. One study found a 12 percent increase in childhood leukemia for every millisievert of natural gamma-radiation dose to bone marrow.[77] Another study examined the mitochondrial DNA of people who live in an area of Iran with high background radiation. This study found that higher rates of mitochondrial DNA mutations correlated with higher background exposure and that mutations were transmitted across generations:

> The observation that radiation accelerates point mutations at all is unexpected, at first glance, because radiation was, until recently, thought to generate primarily DNA lesions. A potential explanation is provided by our additional observation that these radiation-associated point mutations are also evolutionary hot spots, indicating that the radiation indirectly increases the cell's normal (evolutionary) mutation mechanism.[78]

This study concluded that mitochondrial DNA was particularly vulnerable to mutations and suggested it therefore served as an evolutionary "hot spot."

As noted in the 1956 BEAR report, most mutations are not beneficial. Accumulating mitochondrial damage, transmitted across generations, could eventually compromise vital cell energy-production functions. Children are at higher risk from radiation exposure, not only because their DNA appears more vulnerable because of more rapid cell division, but also they have inherited all the germ-line genetic damage from previous generations. Taken together these studies demonstrate that common forms of exposure to ionizing radiation can cause cancer and leukemia and that genetic damage can be transmitted across generations. The studies are significant because they suggest that current estimates for dose risks may underestimate actual risks for sub-populations, such as children.

Epidemiological research: Chernobyl

The Chernobyl nuclear disaster, perhaps more than any other event, dramatized the politicization of research on the effects of radiation. On 26 April 1986, block four of the Chernobyl nuclear plant in the Ukraine exploded.[79] Although the amount of radiation releases is still contested, estimates range from a low figure of 50 × 10 to the 6th curies (Ci), or 4 to 5 percent of the total radiation released from the reactor to a high of 10 × 10 to the 9th Ci released, essentially the entire reactor content.[80]

DOI: 10.1057/9781137343123

Fallout occurred across the northern hemisphere, but Belarus, Russia, the Ukraine, Poland, and the Czech Republic were particularly contaminated.[81] The Soviet Union, under the directorship of Mikhail Gorbachev, employed in excess of 500,000 people (mostly USSR soldiers) known now as "liquidators" to combat the radioactive fire. They were eventually successful in containing the disaster after ten days of continuous emissions. 116,000 people were evacuated from the Exclusion Zone, in present-day Belarus and the Ukraine. Today about five million remain in contaminated areas measuring about 37 kBq/m2 of Cesium-137, but ranging upwards above 555 KBq/m2.[82]

The mortality rate from the disaster is still debated. At the third Chernobyl Forum Meeting held in Vienna, representatives from the IAEA, UNSCEAR, the World Health Organization (WHO), as well as government representatives, issued a three-volume report concluding that 9,000 people died or developed radiation-caused cancers with 4,000 children receiving thyroid operations for Chernobyl -induced cancer. These statistics have come to represent the official range of the toll of the disaster, despite the report's acknowledgement of uncertainty at the heart of its findings:

> It is impossible to assess reliably, with any precision, numbers of fatal cancers caused by radiation exposure due to the Chernobyl accident – or indeed the impact of the stress and anxiety induced by the accident and the response to it. Small differences in the assumptions concerning radiation risks can lead to large differences in the predicted health consequences, which are therefore highly uncertain.[83]

Debate is not restricted to the statistical toll of the disaster, but also concerns the level of radiation experienced by workers and civilians. The Chernobyl Forum claims that recovery workers received up to 500 millisieverts with an average exposure of about 100 millisieverts.[84] The "effective doses" (i.e., "overall health risks due to any combination of radiation") to civilians evacuated from the Chernobyl area are averaged at 33 millisieverts with the highest dose estimated at 700 millisieverts.[85] The exposure levels to Chernobyl radiation can be compared to an average global exposure level of 2.4 millisieverts, according to the UNSCEAR.

The people exposed to Chernobyl fallout were not simply subjected to higher atmospheric "background radiation" from the disaster; they also inhaled and ingested radiotoxic isotopes. Chernobyl Forum exposure estimates may fail to adequately account for myriad health effects from bio-accumulation and bio-magnification of ingested radioiostopes across the food chain, particularly of radioiodine, radiocesium, and strontium. In 1962, Harold Knapp described how radioiodine from a single deposition in pasture-land bio-accumulates and bio-magnifies, producing substantial and injurious radiation doses for children consuming milk.[86] Radioiodine bio-accumulation in the thyroid gland can disrupt normal development, in addition to causing cancer.

Some researchers believe that Chernobyl radiation health effects were much greater in variety and quantity than described by the Chernobyl Forum. Alexey V. Nesterenko, Vassily B. Nesterenko, and Alexey V. Yablokov observe in their Introduction to *Chernobyl: Consequences of the Catastrophe for People and the Environment* that former UN Secretary-General Kofi Annan calculated that at least 7,000,000 people were adversely impacted by the disaster.[87] Their own review of 5,000 medical and scientific studies concluded there were 985,000 deaths from Chernobyl between 1986 and 2004, primarily from cancer, heart, and other circulatory diseases, and excess infant mortality. Perhaps most troubling of all, they argue only 20 percent of children living in the Chernobyl contaminated areas of Belarus, Ukraine, and European Russia are considered healthy.[88]

Research from the region suggests Chernobyl radiation bio-accumulated in children's bodies and affected their genomic stability. Yury Bandazhevsky found that children contaminated with Cesium-137 producing 50 disintegrations per second (Becquerels) per kilogram of body weight suffered irreversible heart damage.[89] Anna Aghajanyan and Igor Suskov found that male Chernobyl liquidators and their children had increased aberrant genome frequencies, suggesting transgenerational genomic instability as a consequence of radiation exposure.[90] A 2008 review of findings on genomic damage in children published in *Mutation Research* concluded that Chernobyl radiation exposed children suffered consistently increased chromosome aberration and micronuclei frequency.[91]

Biological effects on health and reproduction from Chernobyl fallout also occurred outside of the region. Data collected on fallout effects in the United States and Germany found measurable risks for human and animal health posed by relatively low levels of exposure to dispersed Chernobyl radionuclides. As mentioned previously, research documented post-Chernobyl mortality increases in infants in Germany[92] and also in the elderly and auto-immune compromised in the United States.[93]

DOI: 10.1057/9781137343123

Dr. Dave DeSante, from the Institute on Bird Populations in California, found newborn bird mortality averaged 65 percent and 100 percent for species whose young fed on the new-growth consuming insects in central California coastal regions.[94] DeSante's findings are consistent with a recent meta-review of studies by Anders Moller and Timothy Mousseau on the effects of increased "background radiation" from Chernobyl, which found "significant negative effects on immunology, mutation and disease frequency" across affected animal species, although radiation susceptibilities varied.[95] Moreover, Moller and Mousseau found species decline and mutations in plants and animals in the Chernobyl region amplified *across time*.[96] They explain in a separate 2013 study that the *"long-term effects of mutation accumulation are more important determinants"* of population size and variety than short-term effects from radiotoxicity (my italics).[97]

The studies examined here – the Yablokov anthology, Gould and Goldman's *Deadly Deceit*, and animal research by DeSante, Moller, and Mousseau – document biological effects at exposure levels not predicted to produce them. The dominant dose-effects models, such as the ICRP, may underrepresent real-world risks posed by ingested and inhaled radioisotopes assimilated into bodily organs, where decay releases beta, alpha, and gamma radiation. Risk can also be underrepresented by reliance on adult reference models and by failure to examine bio-accumulation and multiplicative effects from other toxins that bio-accumulate in the body. Finally, contemporary risk-assessment models may underrepresent the health and reproductive risks of mutation-accumulation across generations. Contemporary findings on de novo, or novel, mutations suggest they play a causative role in childhood diseases such as autism[98] and congenital heart disease.[99] Increased rates of de novo mutations may have significant transgenerational effects.[100] The historical concept of a permissible dose was predicated on fatal cancers in adults and "severe hereditary effects" expressed in their children or grandchildren,[101] rather than long-term analysis of the range of stochastic (i.e., probabilistic) health impacts across multiple generations in increasingly radiotoxic environments.

Studying internal emitters

The research on Chernobyl fallout brings into focus the role of "internal emitters" in causing disease. As explained previously, internal emitters are ingested radioisotopes, many of which can mimic non-radioactive

isotopes assimilated by flora and fauna. Radioactive iodine-131 is an analog for non-radioactive iodine, strontium-90 is an analog for calcium,
and cesium-137 is an analog for potassium. The effects of ingested radioisotopes depend upon their location in organs and tissues, their rate and
form of decay, as well as the chemical properties of the isotope. World
War II- era studies of the biological effects of internal emitters, discussed
previously, were classified for decades and non-classified studies are
relatively few in number. However, in the 1970s a series of studies on
ingested radionuclides were conducted on a colony of beagle dogs.

One study on the ingestion of beta emitters using beagle dogs is
particularly memorable. In 1972 the study was published in *Radiation
Research* by a team of scientists led by H. C. Redman.[102] The study injected
66 beagle dogs, ages 12 to 14 months, with Cesium-137 solutions. Eleven
dogs died less than one year post-injection. The dogs that survived at
one year had been given lower doses. They found 3.8 millicuries was a
lethal dose. Similar research was conducted for strontium.[103] Yet another
study found that "chronic irradiation of the lung" from inhalation of
clay aerosols contaminated with radiocerium "resulted in a progressive
radiation pneumonitis among the dogs".[104] These experimental beagle
dogs did not fare well from their exposure to internal emitters.

In a 2008 academic review of the risks from internal emitter, Harrison
and Day note that currently used risk estimates are mostly derived from
studies of the effects of external radiation, the principal source of information being long-term studies of those who survived the immediate
effects of the explosions at Hiroshima and Nagasaki, in 1945 (the so-
called A-bomb survivors). They go on to state, "Doses from inhaled or
ingested radionuclides were not assessed."[105] Harrison and Day concluded
that limited information exists on the long-term effects of internal emitters. Current models of dose effects on internal organs are ultimately
tentative.

In 2001, the U.K. Environment Minister Michael Meacher established a
Committee Examining Radiation Risk from Internal Emitters (CERRIE).
The committee addressed whether the risk factors based on the A-bomb
exposures – "which applied to short, homogeneous, high external doses
of gamma radiation at a high dose rate" – were also applicable to low-
dose exposures and internal exposures over protracted periods.[106] The
committee concluded "the application of these factors constituted an
important source of uncertainty in dose and risk estimates," although the
data from the A-bomb exposure was considered the best data available.[107]

DOI: 10.1057/9781137343123

This unwillingness to grapple with the uncertainties of internal emitters is significant when one considers their efficacy in producing genomic instability.

Laboratory research on ionizing radiation: genomic instability and bystander and delayed effect

Laboratory research on animals and cell cultures has from the days of Muller's analysis revealed the subtle effects of radiation on human chromosomes. Since a comprehensive review of this research is beyond the scope of this book, this section focuses on laboratory findings on radiation-induced genomic effects. Discussion describes how radiation exposure, particularly through internal emitters, produces genomic instability by damaging DNA directly and/or by altering gene expression epigenetically. These findings suggest that transgenerational inheritance of genomic instability in germline cells could pose long-term reproductive problems.

Laboratory research indicates radiation can kill cells directly or can induce cellular damage through energy deposition and the production of free radicals.[108] DNA can be damaged in cells surviving radiation exposure. DNA damage triggers cellular efforts to restore normal nucleotide sequence and DNA structure by reversing or excising damage.[109] Failures of DNA repair can produce instability in the genome, resulting in cancer and other diseases. Radiation also produces indirect effects as the free radicals it causes attack the atomic bonds of DNA. In sum, radiation exposure can produce genomic instability by increasing the rate of mutations in DNA sequence and expression:

> Genomic instability is an all-embracing term to describe the increased rate of acquisition of alternations in the genome. Radiation-induced instability is observed in cells at delayed times after irradiation and manifests in the progeny of exposed cells multiple generations after the initial insult. Instability is measured as chromosomal alterations, changes in ploidy, micronucleus formations, gene mutations and amplifications, microsatellite instabilities, and or decreased plating efficiency... there are multiple pathways for initiating and perpetuating induced instability.[110]

Germ-line DNA damage (in eggs and sperm) is inherited by offspring, creating transgenerational genomic instability.

Ionizing radiation is radiotoxic because it breaks chemical bonds, knocking electrons out of orbit, thereby destroying the "atomic building blocks" of the molecular elements of life (i.e., DNA). These disruptions adversely

DOI: 10.1057/9781137343123

affect cellular reproduction, resulting in chromosomal rearrangement, cellular transformation, and carcinogenesis, among other effects.[111] Researchers today recognize that these effects can be delayed, affecting the progeny of surviving, radiated cells. Therefore, radiation exposure can negatively alter cellular reproduction by killing and damaging cells directly and by creating *long-term* "genomic instability" (*delayed effect*) in surviving cells.

Furthermore, recent research on the *bystander effect* reveals that the effects of radiation extend beyond the nucleus of directly targeted cells as nearby cells' replication processes can also be altered, although the precise signaling events between cells that initiate and perpetuate alterations remain undisclosed.[112] Findings suggest that bystander effects can occur at low levels of exposure to radiation: "At lower levels, some or all of the effects are likely to have been initiated not by direct radiation effects on the cell, but by the bystander effect, in which radiation damage to one cell can lead to biological changes in surrounding cells."[113] Bystander effects and genomic instability are together referred to as "non-targeted" effects.[114]

All forms of radiation exposure can damage DNA and alter epigenetic signaling. However, ingested alpha particles are particularly effective in producing point mutations in cells neighboring (bystanders of) those transversed.[115] Indeed, the 2006 BEIR report notes that internal alpha particles are more effective than low LET radiation (e.g., gamma rays) in producing genomic instability.[116] Alpha particles are like internal, biologically damaging projectiles:

> a single α [alpha] particle can induce genomic damage in cells that were not irradiated. Since a cell cannot receive a lower dose of radiation during exposure to α particles than a single traversal, these data suggest that at very low radiation doses the genotoxic risk may be significantly underestimated.[117]

Very low levels of exposure to ingested radioisotopes produce high levels of genomic instability. The BEIR concludes, "How this translates into risks of late effects in man is an open question."[118] Alpha emitters such as plutonium that bio-accumulate in organs may therefore pose particularly severe risks, especially when reproductive organs are involved.

In sum, radiation exposure that overwhelms repair mechanisms can result in a cascade of genomic events posing long-term adverse effects for biological health and reproduction. The field of environmental genomics ultimately hopes to explicate the precise relationship between environmentally induced de novo mutations and human diseases and syndromes. The condition referred to as "germ-line mosaicism"

DOI: 10.1057/9781137343123

illustrates broadly the risks of transgenerational transmission of de novo mutations. Germ-line mosaicism, produced by inherited mutations, is characterized by divergent cell populations within an organism and is a known cause of genetic disorders.[119] It is described in the UNSCEAR Report "Heredity Effects of Radiation", published in 2011:

> Germ-line mosaicism (the occurrence of a de novo mutation in a germ-line cell or one of its precursors during early embryonic development), however, will result in a "mutant sector" in the gonad of an otherwise phenotypically normal individual, and such an individual will generate gametes carrying the mutation, which in turn may result in individuals carrying the same mutation in the following generation (mutant clusters).[120]

The report notes that calculations for human mutation rates have yet to be generated but that human germ-line mosaicism risk assessments should be developed. The report also notes that the genetic damage occurring with germ-line mosaicism may not be visible through phenotypic analysis because mutations may affect recessive genes.

Germ-line mosaicism represents the dangers warned by geneticists in 1956. Radiation-induced mutations to germ-line cells impact offspring and although mutations may be recessive, they can impact human health. New research on "epigenetics" indicates that genomic instability can occur in the absence of direct, immediately detectable DNA mutations as a result of oxidative stress, among other influences.[121] The "bystander" and "delayed" effects examine instabilities that emerge over time. Epigenetic and genetic damage caused by radiation exposure can be heritable. Those impacted with genetic damage caused by their parents' and grandparents' exposure to ionizing radiation may themselves be more vulnerable to genomic instability having been "sensitized," particularly when subjected to additional radiation and chemical assaults.[122] The description of Fukushima by Japanese-American physicist, Michiko Kaku, as a ticking time bomb applies to germ-line mosaicism as well.[123] At some indeterminate point, the accumulation of genetic damage could prevent successful human reproduction.

The politics of radiation research

This chapter provides a chronology of how radiation became linked to health risks across the twentieth century. This last section discusses the politics of risk in relation to radiation research. Through accident and

DOI: 10.1057/9781137343123

biological research, it has come to be understood that radiation causes biological harm and may increase risks for disease and reproductive problems. In 1928 it was known that X-rays damaged the chromosomes of fruit flies. By the 1940s it was known that ingested radioisotopes concentrate in the human body, causing wasting disease and cancer. Wartime laboratory research efficiently documented the horrific toxicity of ingested and inhaled radioisotopes. Still later in the twentieth century, environmental science demonstrated how bio-accumulation and bio-magnification together amplify biological risks posed by radionuclides in the environment. Complex animals, such as humans, located at food chain pinnacle were discovered to be at greatest risk.

Growing scientific understandings of the biological risks of radiation occurred as atmospheric testing and the nuclear industry were launched. The 1956 public BEAR report was an unprecedented effort to explore the implications of increased rates of background radiation in the environment. The actual public report and media coverage document geneticists' deep concerns about the risks to human heredity. Geneticists warned that acquired genetic mutations from radiation are heritable through germ-line cells and cumulate across generations. Each new generation acquires their progenitors' germ-line cell mutations. Mutations may remain relatively "silent" or undetectable, exerting negligible or subtle influences on health and longevity. Eventually, however, rapidly increasing levels of mutations may spike disease rates and produce reproductive failures across a few generations. The study warned that no one knows when that will occur.

The 1956 BEAR report begins by noting that although radioactive decay has always existed in the environment, substantial increases in atomic activity could have "profound effects on all forms of life."[124] It concludes by cautioning that all forms of increased exposure to radiation pose genetic risks. Statistical evidence now exists that atomic fallout from atmospheric testing caused increased rates of cancers and leukemia, at relatively low levels of exposure. The number of deaths caused by atmospheric testing is disputed and probably unknowable, as are the deaths and reproductive disorders caused by Chernobyl, Three Mile Island, and many other nuclear accidents. Perhaps the significant increase in "background" radiation has contributed to rising incidents of autism, ADHD, diabetes, and neurological disorders (e.g., Parkinson's and Alzheimer's syndromes) in Western nations.

Today, scientists have new laboratory tools for examining the subtleties of biological risks from radiation. Genetic sequencing technology

DOI: 10.1057/9781137343123

discloses how human DNA is broken when transversed by a single alpha particle. Mutations in genetic code affect cellular reproduction. New assays reveal minute errors in gene expression and protein production caused by de novo mutations and epigenetic changes. Moreover, effects are not limited to cells directly targeted by radioactive decay. Studies of gene expression document deleterious effects in cellular reproduction by "bystander" cells not directly targeted with radioactive decay.

Most contemporary radiation exposure guidelines still presuppose that dose effects are targeted and linear, with higher doses causing incrementally more significant effects. However, new technologies reveal that linear and unidirectional relationships are not always found when gene expression is examined. In particular, findings in the areas of epigenetics and proteomics raise questions about low-level dose effects on genomic instability, particularly at biologically vulnerable periods in development. It seems probable that this research trajectory on nontargeted effects in gene expression will ultimately call into question the predictive value of our current risk models.

What can be concluded more generally is the current risk models may under-predict the incidents and range of diseases caused by radiation exposure, within the individual's lifespan and across generations of their progeny. Bio-accumulation in organs, bio-magnification in predators, synergy effects, and the vulnerabilities produced by increased rates of transgenerational genetic mutations present significant challenges to the ecological validity of contemporary dose-effects models. Furthermore, use of adult male reference models when setting protective action guidelines may be particularly inappropriate because infants and women appear to be more radiation sensitive. Small amounts of radiation may have significant genetic effects at critical developmental periods, especially on synaptic development. One especially relevant finding for human reproductive health is the discovery that mitochondrial DNA is particularly vulnerable to disruption by ionizing radiation, even among people acculturated to relatively high levels of natural (not human produced) background exposure.[125] What might rapid increases in human-produced radioisotopes have on human mitochondrial DNA ? No one knows for sure.

Notes

1   National Academy of Sciences (1956) *The Biological Effects of Atomic Radiation: A Report to the Public from a Study by the National Academy of Sciences.* Washington: National Academy of Sciences-National Research Council.

DOI: 10.1057/9781137343123

2   International Atomic Energy Agency (2012) "A Short History of the IAEA," http://www.iaea.org/About/history.html, date accessed 3 June 2012.

3   D. Fischer (1997) *History of the International Atomic Energy Agency: The First Forty Years*, http://www-pub.iaea.org/MTCD/publications/PD F/ Pub1032_web.pdf, date accessed 23 September 2012.

4   United Nations Scientific Committee on the Effects of Atomic Radiation (2012) "About Us," http://www.unscear.org/unscear/en/about_us.html, date accessed 7 July 2012.

5   National Research Council (2006) *Health Risks from Exposure to Low Levels of Ionizing Radiation: BEIR VII Phase 2*, 323, http://books.nap.edu/openbook. php?record_id=11340&page=323, date accessed 3 September 2012.

6   Wikipedia (2012) "ALARP," http://en.wikipedia.org/wiki/As_low_as_ Reasonably practicable, date accessed 5 September 2012.

7   A. Makhijani (April 2009) "The Use of Reference Man in Radiation Protection Standards and Guidance with Recommendations for Change," *Institute for Energy and Environmental Research*, http://ieer.org/downloads/53, date accessed 30 April 2009.

8   National Research Council, *BEIR VII Phase 2*. http://www.nap.edu/openbook. php?isbn=030909156X, date accessed 9 June 2011.

9   The Nuclear Energy Agency Organisation for Economic Co-Operation and Development 2011 report, *Evolution of ICRP Recommendations 1977, 1990, and 2007*, explains that the ICRP distinguished between nonstochastic (deterministic) and stochastic (probabilistic) effects in 1977, but it didn't provide quantitative estimates of the stochastic risk for fatal cancer across the lifespan and severe hereditary effects from radiation until 1990 (pp. 15–16). The 2007 ICRP publication incorporates "detriment," which attempts to quantify all deleterious effects of exposure by including cancer incidences, not simply fatal cases (p. 16). The models still rely on a homogenized reference man and doesn't address other diseases (available at http://www. oecd-nea.org/rp/reports/2011/nea6920-ICRP-recommendations.pdf, date accessed 22 May 2013).

10 J. Robert and A. Smith (2008) "Conceptual and Normative Dimensions of Toxicogenomics," in J. Grodsky, G. Marchant, and R. Sharp (eds) *Genomics and Environmental Regulation* (Baltimore: John Hopkins University Press).

11 J. M. Gould and B. A. Goldman (1993) *Deadly Deceit: Low Level Radiation High Level Cover – Up* (New York: Four Walls Eight Windows), p. 7.

12 National Research Council, *BEIR VII Phase 2*, p. 323.

13 Ibid.

14 European Committee on Radiation Risk (2010) *The Health Effects of Exposure to Low Doses of Ionizing Radiation*, http://www.euradcom.org/2011/ecrr2010. pdf, date accessed 23 October 2012.

DOI: 10.1057/9781137343123

15 Environmental Protection Agency (1999) *Cancer Risk Coefficients for Environmental Exposure to Radionuclides: Federal Guidance Report No.13*, http://www.epa.gov/radiation/docs/federal/402-r-99-001.pdf, date accessed 25 November 2012.

16 U.S. Geological Survey (2011) *Bioaccumulation*, http://toxics.usgs.gov/definitions/ bioaccumulation.html, date accessed 2 August 2012.

17 Ibid.

18 T. Hirose (2011) *Fukushima Meltdown* (Osaka, Japan: Asahi Shinsho Books), p. 73.

19 A. Hoffman (2008) *The Code Killers: Why DNA and Ionizing Radiation Are a Dangerous Mix: An Exposé of the Nuclear Industry* (Carlsbad: Ace Hoffman), p. 9.

20 C. Pickover (2012) *The Medical Book: From Witch Doctors to Robot Surgeons, 250 Milestones in the History of Medicine* (New York: Sterling Publishing), p. 276.

21 S. Walker (2000) *Permissible Dose: A History of Radiation Protection in the Twentieth Century* (Berkeley, California: University of California Press), p. 1.

22 Pickover, *The Medical Book*, p. 272.

23 Walker, *Permissible Dose*, p. 3.

24 N. Pasachoff (1996) *Marie Curie and the Science of Radioactivity* (New York and Oxford: Oxford University Press).

25 E. Rutherford (1899) "Uranium Radiation and the Electrical Conduction Produced By I," *Philosophical Magazine*, 47.284, 109–163.

26 E. Rutherford and F. Soddy (1902) "The Cause and Nature of Radioactivity," *Philosophical Magazine*, 4, 370–396.

27 R. Macklis (1993) "The Great Radium Scandal," *Scientific American*, 8, 94–99.

28 B. Kovarik and M. Neuzil (1996) "The Radium Girls," *Mass Media and Environmental Conflict*, 32–52, http://www.radford.edu/~wkovarik/envhist/radium.html, date accessed 22 September 2012.

29 H. J. Muller (1927) "Artificial Transmutation of the Gene," *Science*, 46, 84–87.

30 F. Hanson and F. Heys (3 August 1928) "The Effects of Radium in Producing Lethal Mutations in Drosophila Melanogaster," *Science*, 68.1753, 115–116.

31 H. Dunster, B. Lindell, and J. Valentin (1999) *International Commission on Radiological Protection: History, Policies, Procedures*, http://www.icrp.org/docs/Histpol.pdf, date accessed 25 July 2012.

32 E. J. Calabrese (2009) "The Road to Linearity: Why Linearity at Low Doses Became the   Basis for Carcinogen Risk Assessment," *Archives in Toxicology*, 83, 205.

33 Calabrese, "The Road to Linearity," p. 205.

34 W. LeBaron (1998) *America's Nuclear Legacy* (Commack, New York: Nova Science Publishers), p. 14.

35 LeBaron, *America's Nuclear Legacy*, pp. 14–15.

36 G. Mitchell (2012) *Atomic Cover-Up: Two U.S. Soldiers, Hiroshima and Nagasaki and the Greatest Movie Never Made* (New York: Sinclair Books).

DOI: 10.1057/9781137343123

37   E. Welsome (1999) *The Plutonium Files* (New York: Dell).

38   A. Goliszek (2003) *In the Name of Science: A History of Secret Programs, Medical Research, and Human Experimentation* (New York: St. Martin's Press), p. 126.

39   P. Cockburn (1994) "CIA 'Destroyed Files on Radiation Victims," *The Independent*, http://www.independent.co.uk/news/world/cia-destroyed-files-on-radiation-victims-the-public-may-never-know-full-details-of-secret-experiments-on-americans-during-the-cold-war-1397987.html, date accessed 12 June 2012.

40   P. Langley (2012) *Medicine and the Bomb: Deceptions from Trinity to Maralinga* (Aldinga Beach, South Australia: Paul Langley), http://pothi.com/pothi/book/ebook-paul-langley-medicine-and-bomb, date accessed 21 December 2012.

41   J. G. Hamilton (1947) "The Metabolism of the Fission Products and the Heaviest Elements," *Radiology*, 49, 325–343, http://radiology.rsna.org/content/49/3/325, date accessed 27 June 2012.

42   A. Kraft (2009) "Atomic Medicine: The Cold War Origins of Biological Research," *History Today*, 59.11, 172–218.

43   K. Ozasa, Y. Shimizu, A. Suyama, F. Kasagi, M. Soda, E. J. Grant, R. Sakata, H. Sugiyama, and K. Kodama (2012) "Studies of the Mortality of Atomic Bomb Survivors, Report 14, 1950–2003: An Overview of Cancer and Noncancer Diseases," *Radiation Research*, 177, 229–243.

44   Ozasa et al. "Studies of the Mortality of Atomic Bomb Survivors," p. 234.

45   I. Goddard (2011) "Review of data published by the Radiation Effects Research Foundation," *Goddard's Journal*, http://www.youtube.com/user/GoddardsJournal, date accessed 5 June 2012.

46   Shuntaro Hida, a Japanese doctor, has advocated on behalf of atomic bomb victims since Hiroshima and Nagasaki. He explained in a December 2012 lecture: "The term 'internal radiation exposure' didn't exist at the time [wartime].... Because these people entered the city and were exposed to radiation, we called it 'city-entering radiation exposure'. We had no theory on why they were dying, though." In 1950, Hida opened a clinic to treat survivors, many of whom came at night to avoid stigmatization. Hida wrote in his book, *Naibu hibaku no kyoi* [The Threat of Internal Radiation Exposure]: "This is inherited by the second (children's) generation, and the third generation." Source: "Bomb Survivor Doctor Continues to Speak up about Significance of Internal Exposure" (23 January 2012), *The Mainichi*, http://mdn.mainichi.jp/mdnnews/news/20120123p2a00m0na013000c.html, date accessed 25 January 2012.

47   A. Bouville, C. Land, and S. Simon (2006) "Fallout from Nuclear Weapons Tests and Cancer Risks," *American Scientist*, 94, 48–59, p. 50.

48   Bouville, Land, and Simon, "Fallout from Nuclear Weapons Tests and Cancer Risks," p. 48.

DOI: 10.1057/9781137343123

49 R. Plumb (9 June 1955) "Fallout Effects Gone in 6 Months," *The New York Times*, 21.

50 Walker, *Permissible Dose*, p. 20.

51 W. Laurence (1955) "Radiation Expert Warns on Dosage," *The New York Times*, 28.

52 National Academies of Science (2013) "Committees on Biological Effects of Atomic Radiation, 1954–1964," *Organized Collections*, http://www.nasonline.org/about-nas/history/archives/collections/cbear-1954-1964.html, date accessed May 20, 2013.

53 J. Hamblin (2007) "A Dispassionate and Objective Effort: Negotiating the First Study on the Effects of Atomic Radiation," *Journal of the History of Biology*, 40.1, 147–148, p. 152.

54 Calabrese, "The Road to Linearity," p. 208.

55 Hamblin, "A Dispassionate and Objective Effort."

56 A. H. Sturtevant (1954) "Social Implications of the Genetics of Man," *Science*, 120, 406.

57 Hamblin, "A Dispassionate and Objective," p. 165.

58 "Text of Genetics Committee Report Concerning Effects of Radioactivity on Heredity" (13 July 1956), *The New York Times*, 18.

59 The genetics committee consisted of Warren Weaver, H. Bentley Glass, G. Beadle, James Crow, M. Demerec, G. Failla, Alexander Hollaender, Berwind Kaufman, C. C. Little, H. J. Muller, James Neel, W. L. Russell, T. M. Sonneborn, A. H. Sturtevant, Shields Warren, Sewall Wright.

60 Text of Genetics Committee Report Concerning Effects of Radioactivity on Heredity" (13 July 1956), *The New York Times*, 18.

61 National Cancer Institute (2010) *Reducing Environmental Cancer Risk*, http://deainfo.nci.nih.gov/advisory/pcp/annualreports/pcp08-09rpt/PCP_Report_08-09_508.pdf, date accessed 12 July 2012.

62 Simon, Bouville, and Land, "Fallout from Nuclear Weapons Tests."

63 P. Pringle and J. Spigelman (1983) *The Nuclear Barons*, 2nd edn (New York: Avon), p. 315.

64 E. Sternglass (1963) "Cancer: Relation of Prenatal Radiation to Development of the Disease in Childhood," *Science*, 140.3571, 1102–1104.

65 Walker, *Permissible Dose*, p. 37.

66 Ibid.

67 Ibid., p. 39.

68 L. Freeman (1982) *Nuclear Witnesses: Insiders Speak Out* (New York: WW Norton & Co.), p. 100.

69 C. Sermage-Faure, D. Laurier, S. Goujon-Bellec, M. Chartier, A. Guyot-Goubin, J. Rudant, D. Hemon, and J. Clavel (2012) "Childhood Leukemia around French Nuclear Power Plants – The Geocap Study, 2002–2007," *International Journal of Cancer*, 131.5, 769–780, http://onlinelibrary.wiley.com/doi/10.1002/ijc.27425/pdf, date accessed 7 September 2012.

DOI: 10.1057/9781137343123

70   M. Blettner, P. Kaatsch, S, Schmiedel, R. Schulze-Rath, and C. Spix (2008) "Leukaemia in Young Children Living in the Vicinity of German Nuclear Power Plant," *International Journal of Cancer*, 122, 721–726; M. Blettner, P. Kaatsch, S, Schmiedel, R. Schulze-Rath, and C. Spix (2008) "Case-Control Study on Childhood Cancer in the Vicinity of Nuclear Power Plants in Germany 1980–2003," *European Journal of Cancer*, 44, 275–284.

71   I. Fairlie (2009) "Commentary: Childhood Cancer Near Nuclear Power Stations," *Environmental Health Perspectives*, 8.43, http://www.ehjournal.net/content/8/1/43, date accessed 24 August 2012.

72   H. Caldicott (2006) *Nuclear Power Is Not the Answer* (New York: The New Press), p. 13.

73   P. Day and J. Harrison (2008) "Radiation Doses and Risks from Internal Emitters," *Journal of Radiological Protection*, 28, 144.

74   Caldicott, *Nuclear Power*, p. 57.

75   C. Bradshaw and B. Jaeschke (2013) "Bioaccumulation of Tritiated Water in Phytoplankton and Trophic Transfer of Organically Bound Tritium to the Blue Mussel, Mytilus Edulis," *Journal of Environmental Radioactivity*, 115, 28–33.

76   C. Stagner (2012) *Hidden Tritium* (Morgan Hills, CA: Bookstand).

77   University of Oxford (2012) "Natural Gamma Rays Linked to Childhood Leukemia," http://www.ox.ac.uk/media/news_stories/2012/120612.html, date accessed 22 November 2012.

78   S. Lutz-Bonengel, B. Brinkmann, L. Forster, P. Forster, and H. Willkomm (2002) "Natural Radioactivity and Human Mitochondrial DNA Mutations," *Proceedings of the National Academy of Sciences of the United States of America*, 99.21, http://www.pnas.org/content/99/21/13950.long, date accessed 22 October 2012.

79   A. Rosen (2006) *Effects of the Chernobyl Catastrophe: Literature Review*, http://ippnw.org/resources-abolition-nuclear-weapons.html, date accessed 22 September 2012.

80   A. V. Nesterenko, V. B. Nesterenko, and A. V. Yablokov (2009) "Introduction: The Difficult Truth about Chernobyl," in A. Yablokov, V. Nesterenko, A. Nesterenko, and J. D. Sherman-Nevinger (eds) *Chernobyl: Consequences of the Catastrophe for People and the Environment* (New York: New York Academy of Sciences).

81   Rosen *Effects of the Chernobyl Catastrophe*.

82   "Chernobyl Forum Reports 20-Year Findings, Offers Recommendations" (October 2005), *American Nuclear Society News*, http://www2.ans.org/pubs/magazines/nn/docs/2005-10-3.pdf, date accessed 9 May 2012.

83   Chernobyl Forum (2006) *Chernobyl's Legacy: Health, Environmental and Socio-Economic Impacts and Recommendations to the Governments of Belarus, the Russian Federation and Ukraine*, http://www.iaea.org/Publications/Booklets/Chernobyl/chernobyl.pdf, date accessed 20 August 2012.

DOI: 10.1057/9781137343123

84 Ibid.

85 Ibid.

86 S. Kirsch (2004) "Harold Knapp and the Geography of Normal Controversy: Radioiodine in the Historical Environment," *Osiris*, 19, 167–181.

87 Nesterenko, Nesterenko, and Yablokov, "Introduction."

88 Ibid.

89 S. Starr. (2012) "Health Threat from Cesium 1-137," *Japan Times*, http://www. japantimes.co.jp/text/rc20120216a1.html, date accessed 12 July 2012.

90 A. Aghajanyan and I. Suskov (2009) "Transgenerational Genomic Instability in Children of Irradiated Parents as a Result of the Chernobyl Nuclear Accident," *Mutation Research*, 671, 52–57.

91 A. Fucic, G. Brunbog, R. Lasan, D. Jezek, L. E. Knudsen, and D. F. Merlo (2008) "Genomic Damage in Children Accidentally Exposed to Ionizing Radiation: A Review of the Literature," *Mutation Research*, 658, 111–123.

92 See, for example, A. Körblein, and H. Küchenhoff (1997) "Perinatal Mortality in Germany Following the Chernobyl Accident," *Radiation and Environmental Biophysics*, 36.1, 3–7, http://www.alfred-koerblein.de/chernobyl/downloads/KoKu1997.pdf, date accessed 4 March 2012.

93 Gould and Goldman, *Deadly Deceit*.

94 D. DeSante (uploaded 11 March 2011) "Dave of the Institute for Bird Population in Point Reyes, California interviewed in 'Fukushima Fallout – Lessons from Chernobyl by Ecological Options Network'," *YouTube*, http://www.youtube.com/watch?v=1hcBGSr9QGk, date accessed 28 August 2011.

95 A. Moller and T. Mousseau (2013) "The Effects of Natural Variation in Background Radioactivity on Humans, Animals and Other Organisms," *Biological Reviews*, 88.1, 226–254, p. 249.

96 A. Moller and T. Mousseau (2006) "Biological Consequences of Chernobyl: 20 Years after the Disaster," *Trends in Ecology and Evolution*, 21, 200–207.

97 A. Moller, I. Nishiumi, H. Suzuki, K. Ueda, and T. Mousseau (2013) "Differences in Effects of Radiation of Animals in Fukushima and Chernobyl," *Ecological Indicators*, 24, 75–81, p. 80.

98 S. Sanders, M. Murtha, A. Gupta, J. Murdoch, and M. Raubeson et al. (4 April 2012) "De Novo Mutations Revealed by Whole-Exome Sequencing Are Strongly Associated with Autism," *Nature*, 485.7397, 237–241.

99 R. Zaidi et al. (May 2013) "De Novo Mutations in Histone-Modifying Genes in Congenital Heart Disease," *Nature*, 485, http://www.nature.com/nature/journal/vaop/ncurrent/full/nature12141.html, date accessed 29 May 2013.

100 See, for example, Y. Dubrova, M. Plumb, B. Gutierrez, E. Boulton, and A. Jeffreys (4 May 2000) "Genome Stability: Transgenerational Mutation by Radiation," *Nature*, 405, http://www.nature.com/nature/journal/v405/n6782/abs/405037a0.html, date accessed 5 May 2012.

DOI: 10.1057/9781137343123

101   The Nuclear Energy Agency Organisation for Economic Co-Operation and Development 2011 report, *Evolution of ICRP Recommendations 1977, 1990, and 2007*, p. 15.

102   H. Redman, R. McClellan, R. Jones, B. Boecker, T. Chiffelle, J. Pickrell, and E. Rypka (1972) "Toxicity of 137 Cs in the Beagle, Early Biological Effects," *Radiation Research*, 50.3, 629–648.

103   B. Boecker et al. (1970) "Toxicity of Inhaled 9 SrCL in Beagle Dogs. IV," *Fission Product Inhalation Program, Annual Report, Oct. 1, 1969–Sept. 30*, 123–127.

104   R. Pfleger, B. Boecker, H. Redman, J. Pickrell, J. Mauderly, R. Jones, S. Benjamin, and R. McClellan (1975) "Biological Alterations Resulting from Chronic Lung Irradiation: I. The Pulmonary Lipid Composition, Physiology and Pathology after Inhalation by Beagle Dogs of Fused Clay Aerosols," *Radiation Research*, 63.2, 275–298.

105   Day and Harrison, "Radiation Doses," p. 145.

106   Ibid., p. 146.

107   Committee Examining Radiation Risks of Internal Emitters (2004) *Report of the Committee Examining Radiation Risks of Internal Emitters (CERRIE)*, http://www.cerrie.org/pdfs/cerrie_report_e-book.pdf, date accessed 23 August 2012.

108   M. H. Bourguignon, P. Gisone, M. Perez, S. Michelin, D. Dubner, and M. Di Giorgio (2005) "Genetic and Epigenetic Features in Radiation Safety," *European Journal of Nuclear Medicine and Molecular Imaging*, 32.3, 351–368.

109   E. Friedberg, G. Walker, W. Siede, R. Wood, R. Schultz, and T. Ellenberger (2006) *DNA Repair and Mutagenesis* 2nd edn (Washington DC: ASM Press), p. 5.

110   W. Morgan (2003) "Non-targeted and Delayed Effects of Exposure to Ionizing Radiation: I. Radiation Induced Genomic Instability and Bystander Effects in Vitro," *Radiation Research*, 159.5, 567–580, p. 567.

111   L. Huang, W. F. Morgan, and A. R. Snyder (2003) "Radiation-Induced Genomic Instability and Its Implications for Radiation Carcinogenesis," *Oncogene*, 22, 5848–5854,

112   Morgan "Non-targeted and Delayed Effects."

113   A. Hooker, M. Bhat, T. Day, J. Lane, S. Swinburne, A. Morley, and P. Sykes (2004) "The Linear No-Threshold Model Does Not Hold for Low-Dose Ionizing Radiation," *Radiation Research*, 162.4, 447–452.

114   P. Dorfman, A. Fucic, and S. Thomas (7 February 2013) "Late Lessons from Chernobyl, Early Warnings from Fukushima" *Monitor*, 756, 1–19, http://www.nuclearconsult.com/docs/NM_756.pdf, date accessed 14 February 2013.

115   D. Averbeck (2010) "Towards a New Paradigm for Evaluating the Effects of Exposure to Ionizing Radiation Mutation Research," *Fundamental and Molecular Mechanisms of Mutagenesis*, 687, 7–12.

DOI: 10.1057/9781137343123

116   National Research Council, *BEIR VII Phase 2*, p. 70.

117   Morgan, "Non-targeted and Delayed Effects," p. 573.

118   National Research Council, *BEIR VII Phase 2*, p. 276.

119   J. Zlotogora (1998) "Germ Line Mosaicism," *Human Genetics*, 102.4, 381–386.

120   United Nations Scientific Committee on the Effects of Atomic Radiation (2001) *Annex UNSCEAR Report: Hereditary Effects of Radiation 2001*, http://www.unscear.org/docs/reports/2001/2001Annex_pages%208-160.pdf, date accessed 10 October 2012.

121   Through oxidative stress; see Bourguignon et al. "Genetic and Epigenetic Features," p. 358.

122   Ibid., p. 351.

123   M. Kaku (21 June 2011) "Fukushima Still a Ticking Time Bomb," *CNN in the Arena Blogs*, http://inthearena.blogs.cnn.com/2011/06/21/fukushima-still-a-ticking-time-bomb/, date accessed 25 June 2011.

124   "National Academy of Science," *The Biological Effects of Atomic Radiation*.

125   S. Lutz-Bonengel, B. Brinkmann, L. Forster, P. Forster, and H. Willkomm (2002) "Natural Radioactivity and Human Mitochondrial DNA Mutations," *Proceedings of the National Academy of Sciences of the United States of America*, 99.21, http://www.pnas.org/content/99/21/13950.long, date accessed 22 October 2012.

DOI: 10.1057/9781137343123

5
Conclusion

Abstract: *Uncertainty about the scale of the Fukushima nuclear disaster, the manner of fallout deposition, and the dose effects from exposure contribute to the privatization of risks as externalities are experienced by impacted citizens as personal tragedies. Ironically, nuclear has been the crux of security, despite its deleterious effects producing the most profound insecurity within our most basic life processes, within the human genome itself.*

Keywords: Uncertainty of dose effects, vulnerable genome, nuclear decision making, privatization of risks, Mikhail Gorbachev

Holmer Nadesan, Majia. *Fukushima and the Privatization of Risk.* Basingstoke: Palgrave Macmillan, 2013.
DOI: 10.1057/9781137343123.

DOI: 10.1057/9781137343123

Radiation is political, and current governmental and intergovernmental standards of radiation safety reflect the viewpoints of the winners in the 50-year old debate. It may very well be that our genomes are far more vulnerable than accepted standards of exposure presume, particularly when radioisotopes are ingested and inhaled. Who knows what damage has been wrecked upon the collective human genome by approximately 60 years of nuclear experimentation.

Politicization of radiation safety is a Cold War externality that persists today. Ironically, it was "security" itself that pushed efforts to downplay the adverse health effects of radioisotopes. Atmospheric testing in the Cold War was linked to the security of nuclear deterrence. Nuclear plant accidents and routine releases were linked to the security of energy independence. Fallout and nuclear waste were considered acceptable trade-offs by decision-makers. Radiation contamination was therefore an externality of nuclear weapons testing and nuclear energy production. Risk was privatized as the health effects of increased radioisotopes in the environment were absorbed by impacted populations.

The dose-effect models used when weighing nuclear contamination risks reflected compromises between adversarial groups. Consequently, the true scope and range of health risks for nuclear endeavors – from the effects of uranium mining to nuclear waste and fallout – are likely underrepresented, particularly when gestational and generational effects are considered. Yet, it is impossible to exhaustively identify and recognize the full range of risks posed by radioisotopes within and across life spans because of the complexity of modeling environmentally caused diseases. Incalculable risks to personal health and reproduction are therefore privatized and experienced as random personal tragedies, rather than being recognized as systemic externalities.

A nuclear disaster such as Fukushima produces risks that are truly cataclysmic, but also immeasurable. How does one measure the range of diseases that will be caused and/or exacerbated by an increase of exposure to radioisotopes in air, drinking water, precipitation, and food, especially across generations? How does one measure the effects of economic and social dislocation? How does one measure property lost to radiation contamination that has been the basis of livelihoods for generations? How can risk be quantified and managed when so much uncertainty exists? The convergence of cataclysmic effects and immeasurability is particularly devastating for those most directly impacted by such accidents.

DOI: 10.1057/9781137343123

With Fukushima, unanswered questions have direct bearing on long-term health and reproductive consequences:

1　How much total radiation was released into the atmosphere and the ocean from the Fukushima Daiichi plant and other plants damaged in March 2011?
2　How much radiation is now *routinely* being released into the ocean and atmosphere with ongoing cooling efforts at the plant?
3　What is the likelihood of another sudden, large radiation release?
4　How are radioisotopes such as cesium-134 and cesium-137 bio-accumulating in the environment, food chain, and people?
5　What are the health and reproductive risks for populations exposed to the greatest increases in radiation, especially elements such as radioiodine, radiocesium, uranium, and plutonium ?

Repeated power outages for the spent fuel cooling system at Daiichi in March and April 2013 renewed the urgency of these questions.[1] The risks are impossible to calculate. Yet, ultimately, the personal and economic costs of uncertainty are going to be borne by those individuals who inhale and ingest the radioisotopes produced by the disaster, increasing their personal radiological burden and potentially producing germ-line instabilities affecting their progeny. The risks for the collective human genome cannot be represented and so they will never be acknowledged.

Within Japan and abroad, concern has been raised that not enough is being done to protect those who are at most imminent risk. The typically conservative Japanese media have reported on the failures of decontamination of water at the Daiichi site and hot spots in the region.[2] Japanese bloggers, such as Fukushima Diary and Ex-SKF, have helped publicize the human costs of the disaster for English-speaking readers by reporting and translating Japanese news stories, acting as activist citizen journalists. Former Japanese officials, scientists, and engineers have tried to increase public awareness through their advocacy and education, particularly about the need to stabilize the plant. Internet activism is vibrant at sites such as Enenews.com; yet, official action has been slow and inadequate.

UN Special Rapporteur Anand Grover visited Japan in November 2012 to understand "how Japan endeavors to implement the right to health, the measures taken for its successful realization, and the obstacles encountered."[3] He concluded from his visit that more could be done to protect and assist the citizens affected by Fukushima. He expressed

DOI: 10.1057/9781137343123

concerns about the crisis management during the disaster and the subsequent response policies by TEPCO and the Japanese government. He warned of significant radiation contamination and the dangers of internal emitters in food and water. He urged the Japanese government to incorporate citizen radiation findings in decision making about decontamination and exclusions, and he promoted the participation of communities in the health decisions affecting them. It is not clear whether these recommendations will be pursued.

The Fukushima disaster, like every nuclear disaster before it, demonstrates the limits of human control over nuclear technology. Yet, Japan's current leadership, the LDP, continues to see nuclear as the nexus of national security. LDP efforts to protect fuel enrichment at Rokkasho, despite concerns about an active fault under the site, illustrate how calculi of nuclear risk taking are weighted.[4] Government agencies tasked with "security" may prioritize short-term strategic and financial goals over improbable, but cataclysmic, nuclear accidents. Fukushima has demonstrated how this prioritization can persist even in the immediate wake of disaster because of the uncertainties and privatization of risk. *The Asahi Shimbun* reported in February 2013 that a "cozy relationship still exists between nuclear power operators and Japan's new regulatory agency, the NRA."[5] The bonds of this relationship are no doubt cemented in firm financial and military calculi of costs and benefits, while health and environmental effects escape immediate capture in spread sheets and decision making.

Japan is hardly alone in downplaying nuclear dangers and privatizing risks. Today, the Hanford nuclear site in Washington State, employed first during the Manhattan Project to refine uranium and create plutonium, leaks highly radiotoxic sludge into the environment, potentially contaminating much of the Pacific-Northwest of the United States by way of the Columbia River.[6] The public has been warned of no "immediate risk."[7] Mikhail Gorbachev noted in his *Memoirs* that prior to the Chernobyl disaster there had been 151 significant radiation leaks at nuclear power plants around the world.[8] He warned that one or two more accidents would produce contamination far worse than after a nuclear war.[9] Russia and parts of Europe remain contaminated from that disaster, with parts of the Bryansk Region of Russia with median radiation levels of Cesium-137 two orders of magnitude higher than levels of deposition from nuclear weapons fallout.[10] Chernobyl, Gorbachev wrote, "was a bell calling mankind to understand what kind of age we live in. It

DOI: 10.1057/9781137343123

made people recognize the danger of careless or even criminally negligent attitudes toward the environment."[11] Fukushima illustrates that bell call was not heard. How many more bells will ring before humanity has destroyed its ecosystem and genome beyond repair?

Notes

1 M. Fackler (19 March 2013) "Blackout Halts Cooling System at Fukushima Plant," *The New York Time,* http://www.nytimes.com/2013/03/20/world/ asia/blackout-halts-cooling-system-at-fukushima-plant.html?_r=0, date accessed 19 March 2013. Also, see M. Yamaguchi (10 April 2013) "Water, Rats, Outages: Japan Nuke Plant Precarious, *ABC News,* http://abcnews.go.com/ International/wireStory/precarious-japan-nuke-plant-raises-safety-concerns-18921004#.UWbqP8qQN-R, date accessed 11 April 2013.

2 For example, T. Kihara and M. Aoki (17 January 2013) "Crooked Cleanup: Photos, Videos Show Contractors Lied in Decontamination Reports," *The Asahi Shimbun,* http://ajw.asahi.com/article/0311disaster/fukushima/ AJ201301170063, date accessed 19 January 2013.

3 A. Grover (26 November 2012) "UN Special Rapporteur on the Right of Everyone to the Enjoyment of the Highest Attainable Standard of Physical and Mental Health," Mr. Anand Grover: Country Visit to Japan, 15 to 26 November 2012," http://www.ohchr.org/en/NewsEvents/Pages/DisplayNews. aspx?NewsID=12831&LangID=E, date accessed 26 November 2012.

4 "Industry Minister to Continue Nuclear Fuel Cycle Policy" (18 January 2013), *The Asahi Shimbun,* http://ajw.asahi.com/article/0311disaster/fukushima/ AJ201301180037, date accessed 19 January 2013.

5 Jin Nishikawa (2 February 2013) "Nuclear Watchdog in Hot Water over Leaked Report to Tsuruga Plant Operator," *The Asahi Shimbun,* http://ajw. asahi.com/article/0311disaster/fukushima/AJ201302020068, date accessed 5 February, 2013.

6 The Oregon Department of Energy (July 2006) *The Columbia River at Risk,* http://www.oregon.gov/energy/NUCSAF/docs/WhitePaperRev.pdf, date accessed 7 June 2012.

7 G. Botelho (22 February 2013) "Governor: 6 Tanks Leaking Radioactive Waste at Washington Nuclear Site," *CNN,* http://www.cnn.com/2013/02/22/ us/washington-nuclear/index.html, date accessed 25 February 2013.

8 M. Gorbachev (1995) *Memoirs* (London: Doubleday), p. 191.

9 C. Neef (24 March 2011) " 'This Reactor Model Is No Good' Documents Show Politburo Skepticism of Chernobyl," *Spiegel,* http://www.spiegel.de/

DOI: 10.1057/9781137343123

international/zeitgeist/this-reactor-model-is-no-good-documents-show-politburo-skepticism-of-chernobyl-a-752696.html, date accessed 25 March 2011.

10   V. Ramzaev, H. Yonehara, R. Hille, A. Barkovsky, A. Mishine, S. Sahoo, K. Kurotaki, and M. Uchiyama (2006) "Gamma-Dose Rates from Terrestrial and Chernobyl Inside and Outside Settlements in the Bryansk Region, Russia in 1996–2003," *Journal of Environmental Radioactivity*, 85, 205–227, 217.

11   Gorbachev, *Memoirs*, p. 193.

DOI: 10.1057/9781137343123

Index

DOI: 10.1057/9781137343123

Convention on Supplementary
  Compensation (CSC) for Nuclear
  Damage, 78
crisis communication, 2
crisis management, 10, 44, 143

DNA, 5, 7, 53, 79, 105, 107, 109, 116, 117,
  119, 122, 124, 127, 130, 131, 141, 144
  genomic instability, 106, 122, 124, 127,
  128, 131, 142
  germ line cells, 107, 109, 117, 118, 122,
  127, 130, 142
  instability, 128, 129
  mosaicism, 129
dose, 63, 104, 115, 121, 126
  effective, 123
  effects, 4, 102, 103, 104, 105, 106, 112,
  121, 126, 131
  models, 4, 102, 120, 122, 125, 131, 141
  permissible, 52, 104, 108, 119, 120,
  121, 125
  tolerance, 110

Eisenhower, 15, 16, 18
Elliot, David, 15
Enenews.com, 142
EPA, 63
  Protective Action Guidelines, 63
European Commission on Radiological
  Protection (ECRP), 103
European Committee on Radiation
  Protection, 106
evacuation, 8
ex-SKF, 42, 142
externalities, 3, 141

Fairlie, Ian, 121
fallout, 2, 4, 113, 120, 123, 124, 141
  aerosols, 5
  hot spots, 8
  maps, 5, 47
  ongoing emissions, 5, 102
  wet deposition, 43
Fukushima Diary, 51, 142
Fukushima Network for Saving
  Children from Radiation, 53

Fuse, Junro, 70

General Electric, 2, 10, 22, 23
Goffman, John W., 120
Gorbachev, Mikhail, 123, 143
Grover, Anand, 142
Gundersen, Arnie, 38

Hacker, Jacob, 3
Hanford, 107, 143
Hida, Shuntaro, 77
Hirose, Takashi, 107
Hiroshima, 16, 20, 71, 126, 112, 113

ICRP, 8, 79
International Atomic Energy Agency
  (IAEA), 17, 35, 39, 103, 123
International Committee on Radiation
  Protection (ICRP), 7, 52, 103, 104,
  105, 106, 107, 110, 120
iodine, 6, 124, 126

Jacobs, Robert, 43
Jaczko, Gregory, 38, 62
Japan
  Ministry of Economy, Trade, and
  Industry (METI), 21, 24
Japan Atomic Energy Agency, 39
Japan Atomic Energy Research
  Institute, 21
Japanese Atomic Energy
  Commission, 21
Japanese Constitution
  Article 9, 21
Japanese Ministry of Education,
  Culture, Sports and Science
  (MEXT), 47, 48, 51
Japanese Nuclear and Industrial Safety
  Agency (NISA), 21, 24, 47, 103
Japanese Nuclear Regulation Authority
  (NRA), 21, 75, 143
Japan National Diet, 2, 43, 74
  The Official Report of the
  Fukushima Nuclear Accident
  Independent Investigation
  Commission, 2, 43, 44

DOI: 10.1057/9781137343123

DOI: 10.1057/9781137343123

DOI: 10.1057/9781137343123

CPSIA information can be obtained at www.ICGtesting.com
Printed in the USA
LVOW11*1430070314

376484LV00007B/130/P